HOW TO
TALK ABOUT
WINE

Discover the
Secrets of Wine
Ten Minutes
at a Time

BERNARD
KLEM

STERLING EPICURE
New York

STERLING EPICURE
New York

An Imprint of Sterling Publishing
387 Park Avenue South
New York, NY 10016

ISBN 978-1-4027-7735-6 (paperback)
ISBN 978-1-4027-9088-1 (ebook)

Library of Congress Cataloging-in-Publication Data

Klem, Bernard.
  How to talk about wine: discover the secrets of wine ten minutes at
a time / Bernard Klem.
    p. cm.
  ISBN 978-1-4027-7735-6
  1. Wine and wine making. I. Title.
  TP548.K546 2012
  641.2'2--dc23

                                                    2011025446

Distributed in Canada by Sterling Publishing
$^{C}/_{O}$ Canadian Manda Group, 165 Dufferin Street
Toronto, Ontario, Canada M6K 3H6
Distributed in the United Kingdom by GMC Distribution Services
Castle Place, 166 High Street, Lewes, East Sussex, England BN7 1XU
Distributed in Australia by Capricorn Link (Australia) Pty. Ltd.
P.O. Box 704, Windsor, NSW 2756, Australia

For information about custom editions, special sales, and premium
and corporate purchases, please contact Sterling Special Sales at
800-805-5489 or specialsales@sterlingpublishing.com.

Manufactured in Canada

2 4 6 8 10 9 7 5 3

www.sterlingpublishing.com

CONTENTS

On pages 26–69, you'll find chapters that describe the different characteristics of wine as arranged in the usual logical sequence of wine appreciation: we look, we smell, we taste, we swallow, and we evaluate.

You'll also find a selection of descriptive language taken from real wine reviews: basic terms are at the bottom of the left-hand page, while more advanced lingo is at the bottom of the right-hand page.

PART 2

PART 3

ACKNOWLEDGMENTS

One of an author's most enduring pleasures is to acknowledge those who helped bring a book to publication. I am therefore delighted to thank, first of all, Carlo DeVito of Sterling Publishing, who championed me in the belief that I could produce a meaningful introductory work with a light touch; Diane Abrams, my graceful and wise Sterling editor; Katherine Camargo, a wine pro who scoured every word and phrase to help make this a far better book; James Rodewald, who carried out the second copyediting review with equal vigor; and Michael Cea, my gentle but eagle-eyed production editor at Sterling. I am deeply grateful to them, as well as to the Wine Appreciation Guild's Elliott Mackey and Bryan Imelli, who distributed my first wine book and who introduced me to Sterling. Thank you all.

Another pleasure I enjoy as an author is to express my profound gratitude to Steve Lo, MD, my gifted and compassionate hematologist/oncologist who kept me alive these many years so I was able to write this book. He never gave up on me, and in turn inspired me to never, ever, give up either. So I didn't, and I'm still here because of him. Thank you, Steve.

A PEEK AHEAD

This is a useful little pocket guidebook to wine geared to busy, curious, and smart people. Just like you, in fact.

I'll teach you just what you need to know, and nothing you don't, about the nature of wine, countries that make it, soil and climate, vineyards, the most important grapes and the wines they make, why grape-growing and winemaking are so hard, wine bottles, closures, labels, styles and fads, plus other relevant stuff. You'll also discover the reason wine tastes the way it does, and why it reminds us of so many other smells and tastes we've experienced before.

Finally, I'll tell you why wine is healthy, when wine is ready to drink, how to identify faults in wine, how to match wine with food, how to order wine out, how to shop for wine, what to bring as a good guest, and how to think and talk about it. At long last . . . you can start to enjoy wine with a whole new sense of confidence.

Cheers! Á votre santé! Cin-cin! Salud! Skoal! Prosit! L'chayim!

PART

1

*It was the smell of vanilla, champagne,
longing, marzipan, peaches, smiles, cream,
strawberries, raspberries, roses,
melting chocolate, lilac, figs, laughter,
honeysuckles, kisses, lilies,
enchantment, ardor itself.*

—Lily Prior, from her book, *Ardor*

WHAT IS WINE, ANYWAY?

Some people call it the stuff of legends. For the rest of us, it's fruit juice with a kick. (In this book, I define wine as the product that results from fermented *grape* juice.)

In addition, unlike virtually all other kinds of beverages, wine is a living liquid, changing and evolving from its birthplace in a fermentation vat to its final packaging inside the bottle you may be holding this very minute. It can sometimes live over a hundred years, much longer than most of us ever will.

One of the many reasons people feel so intimidated buying or ordering wine is that they haven't learned what's good and what isn't; what goes with what food or what doesn't; what's the right wine to order and drink for a particular occasion.

Relax. All that mystery is about to end with a simple smile on your face, put there because you've gained the confidence to know the white from the red from the pink, the still from the bubbly, the costly from the inexpensive.

Wine need not be so mysterious. People have been drinking it for over eight thousand years. We drink wine because it tastes so good, especially with the food we eat. It was, and is, made to be enjoyed with good food, although some people sip the more rarified stuff all by themselves (the wines, not the people).

Of course, you could drink water with just about anything, but why would you want to, when you could make your mouth much happier with a nice cool Riesling, a frosty Sauvignon Blanc, an earthy Pinot Noir, or a spicy Shiraz? (I, for one, don't walk around sipping from plastic bottles of exotic imported water every few minutes; water is good for cooking, for showering, for brushing teeth, even for giving the lawn and flowers a drink, but it isn't as good as wine is with food.)

In a manner of speaking, listen to your mouth. I know, I know, your mouth isn't all that close to your ears. Still, pay close attention when you eat decent food and drink decent wine with it. When your mouth seems to be pleased with what you put in it, the rest of you has to be, too.

I'll talk quite a bit about strange things like happy mouths, or delighted tongues, or satisfied palates. Basically, these are all ways of saying the same thing: when tasting or judging a wine, give it a fair test by being attentive to what your drinking apparatus is saying. If it's happy, you'll say things to yourself like, "This is good" or "This is really nice" or even "This is wonderful!" If the wine doesn't do much for you, you'll say things like, "I don't care for this" or, worse, "This is just awful!" Which is why there are so many different wines out there begging for your attention. Bottom line: one person's "Yum!" could be another person's "Yuck!" (For example, my *yum* is a lusty dry red Zinfandel, but my *yuck* is a sweet white Zinfandel. Sorry, it's just the way my nose and mouth work.)

Keep in mind, though, that drinking wine is all about pleasure. It's about sharing with family and good friends, good food, good conversation, fun, happy times, and memories to store them all.

By the end of this little primer on wine, you should have enough knowledge and tools to become a confident wine buyer and drinker. Trust yourself to learn the basics so you can go on to a much more enjoyable wine-drinking future.

COUNTRIES THAT MAKE WINE

Most countries in the planet's temperate zones, north and south, can and do make wine, simply because there are so many thirsty adults in our world. The important factors for grape-growing and winemaking are decent soil, lots of warm sunshine, cool nights, sufficient rainfall (or irrigation), loving care in harvesting, skilled winemaking, and a huge amount of luck. Easy, right?

Let's take a quick little tour around the planet to see who's who and what's what. The twelve largest wine-producing countries by volume are France and Italy (still slugging it out for the number-one spot), followed by Spain, the United States, Argentina, China (yes, China), Australia, Chile, South Africa, Germany, the Russian Federation, and Romania. As the world warms up, even cool, wet England is finally starting to produce drinkable wines. Most other countries produce such tiny amounts that the wines never leave home.

Here's a good place to introduce the concept of Old World and New World—grape growing and winemaking have been divided by most wine experts into two worlds: the old and the new. Old World wines come only from Europe, period. New World wines come from everywhere else, such as North and South America, North and South Africa, the Middle East, China, Australia, and New Zealand (these last two being just about the oldest New Worlds imaginable). Also, know that many Old World–style wines are made in the New World, and many New World–style wines are made in the Old World. Confused yet?

Anyway, let's begin: Hugh Johnson and Jancis Robinson, two of the world's top wine experts (both from cool, wet England), declared in their authoritative book, *The World Atlas of Wine:* "It would be as impossible to think of France without wine as it is to think of wine without France." Amen, that. Nearly all wine authorities give France the biggest chunk of their attention, simply because France has such a long and rich history producing both still and sparkling wine, some of it great, much of it good, some just plain blah. The major wine-producing areas, north to south, are Champagne, Alsace, the Loire Valley, Burgundy, Jura and Savoie, the Rhône Valley, the Southwest, Bordeaux, Languedoc-Roussillon, Provence, and the island of Corsica. It's hard to travel in France without passing a nearby vineyard. Many people consider France the king of wine countries, or the queen, if you insist. Either way, France continues to rule the high ground of fine wines.

Next, we go to Italy, which is the second biggest wine producer by volume at this time and which makes many of the world's most drinkable wines. Forget that hideous straw-bottle stuff of years ago; now, Italian wines command some of the highest prices and highest praises of any wine produced anywhere. Like France, you can't travel to any place in beautiful Italy without bumping into a vineyard. As someone said to Kevin Zraly, the renowned wine author and educator: "There is no country. Italy is one vast vineyard from north to south." I'll drink to that. Starting just below the mountainous Alps in the north are the important wine-producing regions of Piedmont, Lombardy, Veneto, and Friuli-Venezia Giulia; farther south are the central breadbasket areas of Emilia-Romagna, Tuscany, Umbria, Le Marche, and Abruzzo; and at the bottom of the Italian boot are Campania, Apulia, and Calabria. Just beyond them to the west are the large islands of Sicily and Sardinia, both wonderful wine producers, especially Sicily. Sometimes in their wines you can even detect a touch of Sicilian volcanic ash from the still-active Mount Etna between Taormina and Catania.

Spain, the current number-three producer, is very much a major force in making world-class wines. It's a huge country with a huge appetite for good wine and food, like its neighbor France to the northeast. The most important wine-producing areas of Spain are Rioja, Priorat, Ribera del Duero, Navarra, and Andalucía, including the renowned Jerez (Sherry) municipality. Try some of today's wines from Spain when you can; it produces a dazzling array from the quite ordinary to the sublime.

Here in the US of A, every single one of our fifty states makes wine, even warm Hawaii (six wineries; can you smell the pineapple?) and cold Alaska (five wineries; I hope you can't smell the grizzlies). The big gun in American winemaking is, of course, the great West Coast state of California, which will probably remain so because of its many incredible grape-friendly climates and soils; California alone produces more than 90 percent of all American wines. Its two magnificent and beautiful side-by-side winemaking regions known throughout the civilized world are the counties of Napa and Sonoma, north of San Francisco. Elsewhere in California, the major wine regions include Mendocino and Lake Counties in the north, the huge Central Coast, the Central Valley, and the Sierra Foothills. The states of Washington, Oregon, and New York are the top producers after big Cal. If you want to visit some of these beautiful and productive wine regions, nothing will outdo the Columbia and Yakima Valleys of Washington State, the Willamette and Umpqua Valleys of Oregon, or upstate New York's scenic Finger Lakes together with the upscale far end of Long Island.

Argentina is a fast-growing producer of wine and, like its European mother country, Spain, offers everything from everyday gulpers to fine sippers. Much of Argentina's output is derived from the Malbec grape planted high up in the dryish Andean valleys near the Chilean border.

China? This vast country has been producing small quantities of wine from grapes for some five thousand years; it's only recently, however, that China has entered the international wine trade, with production, consumption, and exports expanding every year. Just think about it: more than a billion thirsty Chinese clamoring for wine or something like it to drink. The mind boggles.

Australia, of course, continues to produce an ocean of wine—red, pink, white, bubbly, and dessert-sweet—many guaranteed to make you sit up and take notice, with prices that can be almost embarrassingly low. Believe it or not, Australia produces wine almost everywhere on its vast and varied continent, particularly from well-known vineyards along the Margaret River, in the Barossa, Clare, Hunter, and Yarra Valleys; McLaren Vale; the Adelaide Hills; and Coonawarra. Even the remote island of Tasmania produces decent wines.

Chile has also jumped into the modern age of winemaking, producing many very drinkable and affordable wines to please almost any palate. Here, the Casablanca Valley is the major source of some very credible table wines, most at remarkably low prices.

South Africa hasn't been asleep in the vineyards, either; it produces some compelling aromas and flavors in a wide swath of wine types. Much of that country's excellent export wines come from its three major vineyard areas: Constantia, Paarl, and Stellenbosch.

Germany is still an important producer, much of it white wine and more and more every day less sweet, that is, drier. Some believe its Rheingau and Mosel regions still produce the finest Riesling in the world.

The big Russian Federation, together with the former Soviet republics, has always produced wine, although much of it has been of the coarse country kind. However, Russia's wines are improving, like everything else in that vast land.

The Balkan country of Romania has been a growing white wine powerhouse since the end of the Cold War. It produces some very credible vino for domestic and foreign consumption.

Portugal makes a lot more than Port today, including some fine table reds and whites few people know about. Try some and smile.

Greece makes all kinds of wines, usually white, some lightly resinated to prevent spoilage. Its wine is a good match for fresh seafood, feta, olives, salt air, and eternal sunshine. What's not to love?

Some of the best wines in the world still come from Hungary, a smallish landlocked country in Europe famous for its powerful reds (called bull's blood) and the rich, sweet after-dinner nectar called Tokaji (toe-KAY) that rivals the dessert wines of France and Germany. If you get a chance, by all means take a sip or three. (Tokaji is so highly prized that some Hungarians have even asked to be buried with a drop of it on their lips.)

Our neighbor to the north, in the Canadian province of Ontario, also produces some wonderful dessert sippers, including ice wines that some think are every bit the equal of the renowned German Eiswein (same grapes and type, different spelling).

Tiny (and hot) Israel, of all places, has a modern developing wine industry in the mountains that produces many quite good dry wines, not all kosher. Try some with a belly-busting traditional holiday meal.

Little New Zealand, in the South Pacific nearly 1,500 miles (2,400 kilometers) from its closest neighbor, giant Australia, produces some great reds from the Hawke's Bay region in the middle of the North Island. New Zealand is also a white wine powerhouse, particularly its feisty Sauvignon Blanc from the northern tip of the South Island's Marborough region. The Central Otago region toward the bottom of the South Island is the world's most southerly wine-growing region; it produces some very fine Pinot Noir. (Try, if you can, to find some of actor Sam Neill's Two Paddocks from the Otago Valley—wow!)

Should you really want to challenge yourself, you should learn that almost every country in the world makes some sort of wine, even the tiny near-frozen island of Iceland in the cold North Atlantic.

Right now, however, just know this: there are thousands upon thousands of wines out there from hundreds and hundreds of wine-producing regions around the world . . . just don't expect to experience most, or even many, of them in your lifetime. No one will ever live long enough, including you and me, to work our way through the dizzying surfeit of wine available. Just try as many as you can and let your enjoyment and appreciation grow over time. Now, let's get on to what grapes grow in, plus some of the many things that influence the taste of wine.

A REIGN OF *TERROIR*

Soil is dirt; dirt is ground; ground is earth. Some humus, some sand, some stones, some moisture, some creepy-crawly critters, all of which comprise the thin crust of our unique island planet called Earth.

However, *goût de terroir* (goo duh ter-WAH), which means "taste of place" or "taste of earth" in French, is a very different can of worms. This *terroir* word, from the French who know a thing or two about wine, has baffled wine lovers (mostly non-Europeans) for ages. Why? Because the French believe that *terroir* is the soul of the land, the almost indefinable essence of a particular piece of ground, a serious sense of place, what one wine expert has called *somewhereness*. The controversy as to whether *terroir* exists or not continues on, with no agreement in sight. Let's just say the concept is still contested by *terroirists* and non-*terroirists* alike.

Don't get caught up trying to understand all the subtleties of *terroir*. For the vast majority of wine drinkers, it's easy to recognize that grapes are just another agricultural product, like wheat, corn, tomatoes, and strawberries. They all taste the way they do because of their genetics and that very piece of earth they came from.

Only experienced drinkers usually detect *terroir* in wine, not casual wine drinkers like us. Simply appreciate that the wine we're drinking has a taste of place, that nowhere else in the world makes wine exactly like this one.

In fact, we only need the strength to pull the cork or twist off the cap to begin enjoying one of the greatest gifts of the Earth known to humankind: wine.

THE WRATH OF GRAPES

There are some places on this planet Earth where you can plant a few seedlings in the ground, walk away, and return months or even years later to find fruits and vegetables thriving. Wild grapes are an example; cultivated wine grapes are not.

Given the right conditions, however, wine grapes can prosper; they can also wither and die just as easily. It's best, therefore, to know which grapes are good for turning into wine.

Experts tell us there are some eight-to-ten thousand different kinds of grapes grown today, including all the varieties, hybrids, clones, even clones of clones, plus other genetic modifications. All major wine grapes today were domesticated from wild grapes, but still come in just two basic colors: white (actually a pale yellowish-green) and red (light to dark to almost black).

What about rosé (rose-AY), and how does it get to be pink? Is it made from pink grapes? No. Rosé wine is traditionally made by removing the red grape skins (that contain the color) from the fermenting grape juice after a short period so only a small amount of grape skin pigment colors the juice. There are some impatient vintners who simply blend red and white wines to get something like rosé, but that's not the genuine article. As for rosé lovers, most drink it only during warm weather; some, like my wife, prefer it all year round.

However, and it's a big however, if you plan to master the principles of wine, even the basics, you should try to learn to pronounce and remember grape names. In this case, simply memorize the eighteen classic grapes that make almost all wine today. You can read about the other hundred or so wine grapes elsewhere.

The eight most important *white* grapes used to make wine are:

Chardonnay (SHAR-don-ay)

Chenin Blanc (shen-in-BLON)

Gewürztraminer (gir-VIRTZ-tram-een-er)

Muscat (moos-CAHT)

Riesling (REESE-ling)

Sauvignon Blanc (so-vin-yon BLON)

Sémillon (say-me-YON)

Viognier (vee-on-YEAY)

The ten most important *red* grapes used to make wine are:

Cabernet Sauvignon (cab-er-NAY SO-vin-yon)

Garnacha Tinta (gar-NASH-a-teen-ta) or
   Grenache Noir (gren-AHSH nwahr)

Merlot (mare-LOW)

Nebbiolo (neb-bee-OH-lo)

Pinot Noir (pee-noh NWAHR)

Sangiovese (SAN-ge-o-vayse-ee)

Syrah/Shiraz (sear-AH/shear-AAZ)

Tempranillo (temp-rah-NI-oh)

Zinfandel (ZIN-fan-dell)

If you have trouble pronouncing these names, go find someone more knowledgeable about wine, have him or her pronounce the names for you, and listen closely. If you can't find anybody to help, simply go into an empty room, close the door, and walk around with this list, pronouncing them as best you can. You can do it if you really try.

Once you master these names, you'll finally be a player in the wine game. So learn them well, even if you failed foreign languages at school.

After you've mastered the names of these major grapes well, no one will ever laugh at you again. Ever. I promise.

YARDS OF VINES

Surprise! The vineyard is any place where grape-vines grow. All over our planet, vineyards are everywhere: in the deepest valleys and on the highest hills, in flood plains and deserts, even on the hot sides of still-active volcanoes.

All vineyards have only one purpose: to grow vines that produce grapes to be eaten out of hand or made into wine. So far, so good.

Sure, you can grow grapes in your backyard and turn them into wine. That's a hobby. However, you need serious acreage to make wine on a commercial basis. If you've got the financial wherewithal, by all means go for it. (Just remember the old joke about the real cost of owning a vineyard: "To make a million dollars in this business, start out with five million.")

Even owning a vineyard without a winery, growing grapes is a tough job just fighting the soil, the rain, the freezes, the bugs, the birds, the other critters, and just about everything nature can throw at the vineyard. Being battered by hail just before the harvest is only one of the common disasters. Yet, if everything does work out, a really good harvest is the only real reward.

As a wine newbie, you probably don't have to know anything yet about stuff like soil analysis, trellises, canopies, row and leaf density, pruning, irrigation, pest control, and all the other issues you need to address to make a vineyard produce grapes to be turned into drinkable wine. Just sip the final liquid made by others and marvel at the people the world over who do this for a living, usually by choice. They all deserve our thanks.

HARVEST MOON, ER, TIME

There's a nip of fall in the air, the leaves are starting to turn, and almost all the grapes look ripe and ready to harvest. Call out the pickers: it's time to bring in this year's crop of grapes for processing into wine. *Vendange* (French for "grape harvest") is here!

There are few jobs around the world as hard as picking grapes: bent over most of the time, you clip the bunches; place them in a bin; carry the heavy, full bins to a truck or tractor; dump them in; and then start all over again, from sunrise to sunset. (To pick the grapes for Eiswein/ice wine, you go out in the below-freezing middle of the night in midwinter.) Sounds like fun, right? Maybe, if you do it once in your life, fresh out of college just to experience it, maybe it is. Otherwise, it's miserable, hard, backbreaking work, all done by countless thousands upon thousands of men, women, and children around the planet.

Late summer or fall around vineyards is the busiest season of all. In between the storms and all the other hazards, grapes are picked before they rot on the vines. People who run vineyards call it the most exhausting madness anywhere, simply to bring in the grapes to make the wine that makes our dinners so wonderful and makes us happy just to be alive. There are many places where machines do the picking in place of people; however, they're never used for better wines, clusters of which must be carefully picked and sorted by hand.

TIP: Don't pay too much attention to good and bad wine vintages at this time. Just concentrate on buying wines from producers who make good stuff virtually every year.

TURNING GRAPES INTO WINE

Madness comes in many forms. Turning grapes into wine is one of them, at least according to some of the people who do it for a living.

If you want to experience heartbreak firsthand, plant some quality wine-grape plants (especially Pinot Noir, often called the *heartbreak grape* for good reasons). Cultivate them carefully; nourish them with a bit of fertilizer and some water from time to time; let them soak up warm sunshine like a lizard on a rock; wait until the grapes are perfectly ripe; then carefully pick the bunches overlooked by the birds and other wild grape-lovers and transport them to the winery.

Now what? Now, you dump everything into monstrous ugly machines unpoetically called destemmers and crushers that squeeze the pulp to death so that the juice can be pumped into giant fermentation tanks. Usually you add some special yeast to the tanks to start the fermentation process. And boy, does it start: bubbling, gurgling, hissing, and making embarrassing sounds that should never reach human ears in polite company. The fermenting mess gets stirred and often punched down below the bubbling surface with a big flat paddle, after which the whole liquid mess is pumped out into other vats or barrels to await testing and filtering (most wine drinkers don't want to drink the stuff with any crud still in it).

If all goes well, you let the liquid sit for a good while longer before pumping it again either into more barrels for further aging, or into clean, sanitized bottles, to be sealed, labeled, and then held for either more aging or shipped to distributors who reship it to retailers who sell it to you.

Then you cross your fingers and hope people like and buy the wine. Is this not madness?

HOMEMADE VINO

Making wine isn't easy, or cheap, or totally soul-satisfying. Yet, thousands of grape growers and winemakers persist, sometimes against all odds, to produce that singular wine they're proud to call their own. If you're still intent on growing grapes and/or making wine at home, go for it.

You won't be alone.

If you simply feel compelled to become a vintner but don't have the big bucks to do it commercially, you can always join the untold thousands of people who make wine at home in their sheds, garages, basements, teepees, yurts, whatever. They buy the grapes, or the concentrated grape must (the mixture of grape juice, stems, skins, seeds, and pulps resulting from the crushing stage), or even the raw grape juice to turn into wine. They sometimes make a decent drink and offer it to friends, relatives, or anyone who'll try a glass. They're usually very proud of their results, even if it's not up to competition-class standards. Still, they do go on year after year because they love the challenge and sometimes the fine results they get.

If making wine at home interests you, just make sure you get permission from both your state and the federal government if you plan to sell any of the wine, or even transport it to contests or exhibitions; it's a ferociously controlled business. Also ask your spouse or partner to agree to your new passion; home winemaking isn't just an expensive hobby, it's quite a messy one as well.

But don't give up. There are few pleasures in life that'll mean so much as a friend or relative telling you honestly that the stuff you made is good—really, really good. Fabulous even. As in: "How about we pull the cork on a bottle of last year's fabulous *Château Me*?" (Here's my glass.)

BOTTLES, CLOSURES, AND LABELS

History accounts for the different shapes of wine bottles, such as those from Burgundy, Bordeaux, Champagne and Alsace in France, and those from Germany. There are many others, but there's no need to remember them all.

The Burgundy bottle has a sloping shoulder, the Bordeaux a high one, the Champagne a middle-aged spread, and the Alsace a tall, slender shape like its German relatives across the border. For your purposes, wine bottle shape doesn't matter as much as your own shape.

Closures are the little things at the top of the bottle that seal the wine in. Traditional closures, below the foil seal or cap, are made of cork—round plugs from renewable cork tree bark, which, of course, was alive at the time. Artificial corks made of plastic are cheaper to make and in widespread use, but sometimes harder to extract.

The biggest deal in wine closures these days has to be the screw cap, the ubiquitous twist-off top that also seals so many drinks and other household products. Every day, more and more wineries are switching to the screw cap from cork as they find out that screw caps rarely contaminate the wine as some nasty corks do. (Australia now bottles about 75 percent of its wine in screw caps.) However, the verdict is still out on whether screw caps over the long term help promote aging and longevity.

There are a variety of ingenious closures that may or may not seem all that appealing or even romantic. How about the famous Tetra-Pak, the kind with a spout like the one on many juice and milk containers. (Once I found a quote that says, "Wine is the milk of old men.")

There's even a new one called *Zork* from Australia that opens with a plastic peel-around that covers the removable, and resealable, closure. This is a nifty but slightly more expensive invention to challenge the inexpensive screw cap. (For the record, there's also a strong new Zork resealable closure for sparkling wines.)

Some of the most famous of all wine closures are the fat, tapered natural corks that stopper almost all Champagnes and many other sparkling wines. They're made extra strong because of the high pressure of the carbonated wine within. After you undo the wire and the metal cap, you very carefully start to wiggle or twist the bottle to extract the fat cork. When you do this slowly and carefully (pointing it away from any living thing), the cork comes free and makes a sound like a sigh, a very contented one. When you yank it out forcefully, however, it always makes a big festive pop accompanied by a spray of the liquid contents, the signal for the fun and celebration to begin.

That pop could announce the beginning of a new relationship, a seduction, an engagement, a wedding, the birth of a baby, a college graduation, a promotion, a retirement, a boat christening, a winning championship game, even the completion of a wine book manuscript like this one. Whatever it is, enjoy the sound and the bubbly inside before it goes flat. And it will go very flat in time, usually sooner than later. Guaranteed.

Labels, however, can also be confusing. There are usually two important ones on every wine bottle: the front label, always required by law, and the back label, which may or may not be optional, depending on national wine bottling laws. The front tells you who made the wine, and where, and when it was bottled; it also sometimes tells you what kind of grapes went into the wine, all of one kind or a blend of different varieties. The back label usually carries some boilerplate government warning about alcoholic consumption plus some long-winded marketing hype.

Still, look at all wine bottle labels carefully before buying. It's wise to pay attention to the labels just enough so you can figure out what's in the bottle before opening it.

You should also realize that American and most other New World wine labels tend to be straightforward and easy to grasp, while European/Old World labels tend to be busy with lots of words, many unpronounceable, especially traditional German, Austrian, and Swiss ones. It's best to have a wine store pro help you out on these. Don't get discouraged, though, simply because you can't understand the printed words. It's really the good stuff inside that counts.

One of the newest developments in bottle labeling now starting to appear is a German trade group effort, called the Riesling Taste Profile, to indicate the degree of sweetness of each wine. The new label, usually on the back, shows a horizontal graphic that displays the sweetness level: empty or no sweetness on the far left, lots of residual sugar or very sweet on the far right, off-dry or medium dry/medium sweet in the center. This is very helpful to wine buyers who either don't speak or don't comprehend the foreign labels, or who simply want to find out the degree of sweetness inside before they buy. Get into the habit of reading labels. Some will be beautiful, some ugly, some helpful, some just plain silly. Still, good label-reading skills will help you to become wine-smart.

WINE STYLES AND FADS

Like clothes, food and wine share similar ebbs and flows of fashion. Dry/sweet; light-bodied/full-bodied; young/mature; red/white; still/bubbly; Old World/New World; traditional/international. So many wines, so many kinds. It's all so confusing. But wait, all is not lost. Just learn what these words mean and you'll get much more comfortable with the goings-on in the world of wine.

How on earth can wet wine be dry? You'd be amazed how many people ask that very question. The answer is simple: in wine language, *dry* means *not sweet,* that is, *no sugar,* at least no perceptible sugar. *Sweet* is, well, *sugary,* the very opposite of what *dry* means in wine. For the record, no one has really figured out just how dry or sweet a wine should be, other than to measure the so-called residual sugar (sugar left after the yeast has fermented) with complex scientific instruments we don't have to delve into here.

Very generally speaking, white wines and rosés tend to be light, or light in weight; red wines, especially full-bodied reds, tend to be heavier, even heavy.

Wines that were bottled a year or three ago are called *young,* followed by older wines that are called, ahem, *mature.* Try to remember that almost all wines are drunk fairly soon after their first shipment to stores for sale. Better wines are usually aged at the winery before shipping to the market for sale, and are therefore quite a bit more expensive. Well-fixed wine lovers and collectors also further age their wines in their own personal cellars. Nice if you can afford them.

Wine fads are constant, annoying, and sometimes downright silly. A few years ago, everybody was asking for California Chardonnay, the woodier, the better. Today, the pendulum seems to have swung the other way: lots of folks seem to be asking for less or no oak. Hang on; that will likely change again soon. See pages 56–57 for more on wood.

Most people drink still wines (no carbonation) day in and day out, while we tend to drink sparkling wine, such as Champagne, on special occasions. More and more people love to drink Prosecco, a tasty food-loving young sparkling wine from northeastern Italy, or a delicious Cava from Spain. There are also some fine sparkling wines made right here in the States; try some soon. Actually, quite a few wine lovers drink sparklers exclusively, all the time, with all kinds of foods, and on all kinds of occasions. Fewer choices, but many more bubbles.

Traditional wines, by definition, are made the old-fashioned way, sometimes under less than sanitary conditions and with little science involved. International wines are usually made in modern, clean wineries and are intended for the wine drinker who doesn't particularly care where the wine is from or who made it.

If you have an urge to start keeping wine at home (cellaring), all you need is to find something you like and can afford. Then buy a case or two and park them in a dark, cool, and vibration-free place to wait until you pull out a bottle or two to enjoy.

There's really no right or wrong when it comes to wine styles or fads. Like most foods, clothing, makeup, and entertainment, wine is subject to the push and pull of fashion. Still, once you're more comfortable with wine, you can just drink what you like and let others drink what they like, no matter which way the fashion tides are ebbing or flowing.

SMELLING AND TASTING WINE

For the record, you ought to learn one fundamental rule here: the expression *wine tasting* should really be called *wine smelling*. In order to taste, we must be able to smell first. That's the way we're made (our sense of smell is much keener than our sense of taste; some experts put smell as being about 80 percent of taste). According to Diane Ackerman, a gifted student of the senses, some experts have said that wine is simply a tasteless liquid that is deeply fragrant. Perhaps, perhaps not. It's also why we can't taste, let alone smell anything, when we have a head cold. And another thing: never just gulp wine down before smelling it; wine isn't like iced tea or some diet drink. It's complex, subtle, and evocative of more things than you can imagine.

Don't be shy; just stick your nose (beautiful or ugly, nobody cares what it looks like) deep inside the bowl of the glass with a little wine in it (never more than a quarter full) and take a few really good strong sniffs. Inhale deeply and try to identify the scents in your memory bank. Vanilla? Wood? Grass? Sandalwood? Old socks? A haystack? Rover, your childhood dog? Damp earth? The gym locker next to yours? Your lover's sun-warmed skin? A just-bathed baby? Fresh-squeezed grapefruit juice? A flower store? An apple orchard in the fall? There's simply no end to the many smells and tastes that wine produces for you to discover, especially if the sensation is already in your memory bank.

Wine is a magician of aromas and smells. It has the ability to conjure up all kinds of memories, good and bad. Moreover, it does it all through the magic of complex chemistry that's too detailed to go into here. What you smell in the wine isn't really in the wine. It's simply produced by chemicals that smell just like the things they mimic. There are no roses in wine, just some organic smell of roses. The same with apples, or black pepper. Or just-squeezed citrus. Or an old barn filled with warm, freshly mown hay.

Okay, you've gotten a few good sniffs in. Now what? Swirl the wine around in the glass to release more smell and taste molecules so that you can enjoy them. (Try not to splash the wine around you, annoying people wearing expensive, light-colored clothing.) Now, sip a little and taste the liquid, just enough to swish around in your mouth, all around, and then swallow. Did you taste anything you remember? Did it tickle? Burn? Pucker up your mouth? After a moment or two, can you still taste it after it slid down your throat? That's a good thing. See pages 66–67 for more on finish.

You also don't need to gargle wine like some noisy experts. Nor do you have to hiss like a snake when you pull air into your mouth to aerate the wine. In addition, you certainly mustn't spit unless you've already practiced in the bathtub with no one around to shriek with horror or sputter with laughter.

That's pretty much it. You've looked at the wine, you've sniffed it deeply, you've swirled it, you've rolled some around in your mouth, and then you've swallowed it. Not so hard, right? Please don't forget to smile once you get the hang of it.

Learn the basics, the very elementary skills you need to enjoy wine at home, at a dinner party, in a restaurant, on the beach, at a picnic, somewhere romantic with that special person in your life. Wine and romance have been partners since the beginning of recorded history. After an intimate meal with good food and good wine, followed by an evening of further intimacy, you'll figure this all out.

PART

2

*It is well to remember the
five reasons for drinking:
the arrival of a friend,
one's present or future thirst,
the excellence of the wine,
or any other reason.*

—Latin Proverb

I CAN SEE CLEARLY:

To some people *clarity* means just that: it's clear. In a wine context, clarity also means you can see through the wine unless it's so dark as to be nearly impenetrable. It also means there's nothing floating around in the liquid, other than occasional bits of cork that broke off while opening the bottle. In this case, a tiny piece of cork is usually harmless (unless you're allergic to cork, which is very rare).

Still, when you hold up your glass of wine and see through it to something beyond, that's a good thing to many people. It says that the wine has been filtered to get rid of any nasty little bits that shouldn't be there.

Clarity in wine also means brightness, or the lack of it. Don't fret too much about this quality; a lot of people don't quite get what a bright wine is, nor must they. This is simply one of those wine-expert things.

To help you understand the concept of clarity, think of the difference between fresh, clear (filtered) apple cider and cloudy (unfiltered) apple cider. Does the unfiltered taste better than the filtered? It does to some people, but not all. The very same with wine. Clear, huh?

SOME BASIC TERMS FOR CLARITY:
bright, brilliant, cloudy, dark, dingy, drab, dull, gauzy, gloomy, hazy, inky, luminous, lustrous, milky, mucky, muddy, murky, opaque, sedimented, sheer, transparent

CLARITY

In the good old days, say, before 1950, many, possibly most, wines were not filtered very widely. Few people seemed to care whether the wine was clear or not, as long as it gave them the buzz they wanted. Whatever came out of the barrel or cask was what they drank. And enjoyed.

Only later did wine drinkers get uppity and demand that their wines be as clear as water from a cold, running stream, meaning no foreign objects, no floating thingies. Nowadays, however, nobody seems to mind about little bits of floating cork on the surface. Just pick or spit them out (politely).

Today, virtually all wines are filtered, some heavily, before release to the market. There are exceptions, however: unfiltered wines persist because certain winemakers refuse to clarify their product for fear of stripping out the full aromas, flavors, or even textural quality. Therefore, it's the consumer's call—that is, your call—as to which type you prefer, filtered or unfiltered.

Personally, I suppose that any wine you like is the wine for you, so it's okay as long as you don't see teeny-tiny critters doing backstrokes across the surface of the wine in your glass. 1–2–3–4, 1–2–3–4, 1–2–3–4.

SOME ADVANCED LINGO FOR CLARITY:
unexpectedly muddied, looks like the North Atlantic, opaque black elixir, as inky and dark as an octopus wine, so dense you need x-ray vision to see through it

HUE AND CRY:

The color of wine reveals some crucial information: its origin, the grapes used to make it, its age, its general state of health, and sometimes even its quality.

Wine comes in three basic colors: red, pink (rosé), and white. As living liquids, wines change over time, just as we do. Really, it's true. Be relieved that you won't be required to remember all the biology and physics you took in school just to figure out how this works.

Most young white wines can be as light as water; that is, they have almost no color. Usually, these are the whites fresh out of the fermentation tank and straight into the bottle. With time, however, all whites get darker and develop more color, such as a deeper yellow, or gold, or just enough tint to confirm that they're on their way to maturity and beyond.

Red wines are quite purply when young, become more cherry-red or rubylike as they age, and take on a somewhat brownish-red cast as they get close to the end of their lives. Don't worry too much about color unless your wineglass has a garish green, metallic blue, or fluorescent orange liquid in it. Then, you have a good reason to run around and scream bloody murder.

Look at your wine carefully before you smell or taste it. It's part of the wine-tasting ritual, and a very important one.

SOME BASIC TERMS FOR COLOR:

black, blonde, brick, brown, cherry, citron, dark, gold, green, inky, lemon, magenta, olive, pink, plum, purple, red, rose, ruby, scarlet, straw, sunset, tawny, violet, yellow, young

COLOR

Once you've experienced quite a few different wines, you'll notice that wines made from different grapes can and do vary in characteristic color, and that a producer's wines from different vintages can also vary in color from year to year. Keep an open mind and mouth.

As a new wine drinker, you'll rarely run into a weird-colored wine, especially since you'll probably be drinking inexpensive stuff for a while. If you happen to encounter a wine with what you think is a strange color, ask someone more experienced if it's okay to drink.

It's quite important, however, to remember that color is a prime identifier of wine. Expect to be confused occasionally, since some wines look light but are powerful; some will look dark but taste light, some will look like they were made from one grape but they were actually made from another, and some flawed wines will have a color that looks just fine. Many of these aberrations will be sorted out once you take some deep sniffs to check out what's in the glass.

Wine is one of very few living liquids, so it shares some of the same characteristics as living solids, just like us. People have good and bad color; so do wines. Just like people, some wines are healthy-looking and some aren't. Stay alert and take your vitamins.

SOME ADVANCED LINGO FOR COLOR:
squid-ink black, blacker than the devil's heart, like looking into space, Darth Vader®-dark, Aztec gold, inky abyss, ballsy deep purple, girly-whirly pink, ruby slipper, mellow yellow

BUBBLE BATH:

How would you like to relax in a tub full of warm Champagne? All those tiny little bubbles tickling everywhere . . . oh, yes!

Nice work if you can get it. For the rest of us, though, we drink the bubbly stuff, sometimes as an aperitif, but more often on some festive occasion when the pop of a cork marks the beginning of something special. All carbonated wines (from carbon dioxide, silly) are just sparkling wines, without exception. Even Champagne is only another sparkling wine, except its name is protected under law by the French government to indicate the region in France called *Champagne*, about 90 miles (145 kilometers) northeast of Paris.

There are many different sparkling wines: Cava from Spain, Espumante from Portugal, Asti and Prosecco from Italy, and Sekt from Austria and Germany, for example. We even make a lot of sparkling wine right here in America. Almost every country that produces wine makes some sparkling version. How else could we celebrate births, marriages, promotions, winning sporting events, and many of life's other milestones?

Sparkling wines are the unchallenged kings and queens of festive beverages. Drink as many different kinds as you can. See if you don't agree that they're the perfect companions to all our celebrations. End of argument. Cheers.

SOME BASIC TERMS FOR EFFERVESCENCE:
agitated, bubbly, carbonated, creamy, cushiony, effervescent, explosive, fizzy, flat, foamy, frothy, gassy, mousse, pearls, prickly, snowy, sparkling, spritzy, sudsy, tickly, tingly

EFFERVESCENCE

Why is real French Champagne so damn expensive? Because it's made in a slow, costly, and traditional way called *méthode champenoise* (may-TOAD chahm-peen-WAZZ). It's more costly than the methods used to make still wines simply because it requires extra labor and extra time, two good ways to increase production costs. Champagne also has to referment in the bottle (to make the bubbles) after the first fermentation in the tank or barrel takes place. The bottles must be frequently turned (usually by hand) to collect the dead yeast cells inside, which are then extracted by freezing, and finally the wines are rebottled. To some people, the cost is worth it; to others, no.

Not all sparkling wines go through such a complicated and time-consuming process as traditional Champagne. Many are made by means of the more recently developed *Charmat* (shar-MAAT) *Process*, a faster and less costly manufacturing method that accounts for a lot of quite good bubbly.

Real Champagne is made from white grapes, usually Chardonnay; from red grapes, such as Pinot Noir; and often a blend of both, sometimes with added Pinot Meunier, another red Champagne grape.

Nevertheless, let your nose and mouth, and those of your guests, appreciate what's been done for them.

SOME ADVANCED LINGO FOR EFFERVESCENCE:

fierce burst of bubbles, fabulous frothing fizz, frothy sighs, zippy tingle of gas, waves of limpid crystal-line laughter, livelier than a sack full of ferrets

TIME IN THE BOTTLE:

Some people think they get better with age. At what, I ask?

Some people think that wine gets better with age, too. If it's a great wine, that is, expensive and rare, it could, and probably will, improve with age. But only if it's a decent wine, and that's still a *maybe*. Most wines (close to 90 percent) don't get better than when first bought, since they're made to be consumed within one, two, or three years, at most. In other words, don't wait to drink a $10 wine in ten years; it'll probably will have turned to vinegar. Beginning wine drinkers needn't be concerned about the age of wines.

However, if you're determined to see if you can perceive the difference maturity makes in wine, by all means try. It won't be a wasted exercise, since you'll be training your palate to detect the subtle mellowing that some aging can achieve. Drinking a ten- or twenty-year-old wine will certainly open your eyes, so to speak, and help familiarize you with the grace of age.

In the meantime, remember that most of the wines we'll consume over our lifetimes will be young. If you have a well-heeled wine-loving friend who appreciates fine wines that cost more than you usually spend, be nice to that friend and enjoy tasting some well-aged beauties. Your palate should be appreciative.

SOME BASIC TERMS FOR AGE:

needs to age, well-aged, baby fat, backward, well developed, evolved, faded, fresh, green, long-lasting, mature, old old old, opening up, at its peak, promising, tight, young

AGE

I f almost all wines produced and sold today are intended to be consumed fairly soon, what about the remaining wines? Some wines have been cellared for a number of years, and will have some very nice characteristics that aging can bring. It could be your wine epiphany as you savor what time is capable of doing.

How the chemistry of aging wine works is well beyond the scope of this book. Still, you ought to be able to tell the difference between a wine that's a teenager and one that's a full-grown adult, with all that implies. The teenage wine should be perky, fresh, and limber; the adult should be mellow, blended, and balanced (we hope), and should make you sit up and take notice of what time has done to the wine.

For the record, to find a well-aged white wine, look to German and Alsatian Rieslings and French Sauternes; in reds, look to French Bordeaux, Italian Barolos, and vintage Ports. These are just a few examples.

Age in wine is a two-edged sword. Some wines need decades to open up and present their best. Others may be over the hill by the time you get to try them. (Don't make too many comparisons between the age of people and the age of wine, however; age isn't all it's cracked up to be in people. Trust me once again on this one.)

SOME ADVANCED LINGO FOR AGE:
gawky adolescent, whiff of old age, creaking at the joints, embalmed, embryonic, comatose, barely evolved, foot in the grave, immortal wonder, all pooped out, vinous infanticide

ROCK 'N' ROLL:

People don't like the word *acid*. It has a terrible reputation, but in the context of wine, it's an essential component of every wine you'll ever drink. Think of acid as a drizzle of balsamic vinegar on new spring greens; a squeeze of lemon on sautéed fish; a kiss of salt on a perfectly ripe summer tomato bursting piquantly in your mouth. These are all examples of food acids at work. Acid is no less important in wine.

Acidity gives wine its sharpness, its bite, its exhilarating and refreshing taste. Without acid, wine would taste flabby, as dead as a glass of stale water. Which doesn't sound all that attractive, does it? No matter. Acidity in wine is one of its main pillars, along with its vinous companions, such as alcohol, fruit, sugar, and tannin.

In addition, the acidity in wine is what gives it the ability to go perfectly with food. The formula is quite straightforward: high-acid wines pair brilliantly with food (think Sauvignon Blanc with shellfish), while low-acid wines, such as Sémillon or Pinot Blanc, don't work so well.

Be aware also that there are quite a few different types of wine acids, none of which you really have to learn about right now, except that acidity is our friend. Don't be scared of the word *acid;* it's what's in the bottle that counts.

SOME BASIC TERMS FOR ACID:
acetic, brisk, brutal, crisp, edgy, fresh, lively, mouthwatering, nervous, pungent, racy, refreshing, searing, sharp, snappy, sprightly, stinging, tangy, tart, vibrant, zesty, zippy

ACID

If you're looking for a wine that goes great with food, you're in luck. Any wine that's high in acidity will do the trick. Wines with high-acid content are known to cut rich, fatty foods, such as those loaded with a lot of butter and cream.

Which wines, exactly? Riesling, the unchallenged king of white grapes, is the historical leader in this category, because it's as friendly to foods as it gets. Also, Sauvignon Blanc, due to its acidic bite; this is the classic white to drink with most seafood. Champagne and other sparkling wines are other famous marriage partners of food and wine.

In the red-wine category, many people like to drink Cabernet Sauvignon with meats of all kinds. Barbera is also fine with food because it has a high acid content, even though it's low in tannin. Other good food reds are Merlot, Pinot Noir, and Syrah.

Remember that acid is critically important in wine, especially with food, and that wines with high acid are what we call *fresh.* Don't be afraid to experiment. Keep trying different varieties, red and white, still and sparkling, until you get to *yum.*

Keep in the back of your mind, though, that some wines can be too acidic, and can scour your mouth clean like a hit of icy cold fresh grapefruit juice. All of which can lead to the descriptors below. *Skoal!*

SOME ADVANCED LINGO FOR ACID:
buttock-clenchingly acidic, cuts your palate to shreds, tooth-crackingly racy, nose-prickling pungency, like gargling with razor blades, enamel-ripping

HEADY STUFF:

Surprise! Wine contains alcohol, which usually makes most people happy, and that's the reason a lot of people drink it. To many of us, the fact that it also tastes good is a big bonus.

On the other side of this coin, many people simply like the taste of wine, and the fact that it happens to contain alcohol, which also makes them happy, is another bonus.

Either way, the alcohol in wine separates it from mere grape juice, which anyone can make simply by squeezing ripe grapes.

Alcohol is the end product of the fermentation of the natural sugars in grapes. Most wines have between 8 and 16 percent alcohol, enough to get a buzz on if you only drink two or three glasses; if you drink more, the alcohol will start to affect your speech, your vision, your stability and your perception. Always keep this in mind if you're either the designated wine drinker or the designated driver.

Yet, alcohol also contributes to wine's reputation as a healthy beverage if taken in moderation. A little (one to two glasses) every day is good for you; more is not.

Also, remember that alcohol, like so many other components of wine, should be in balance with other vital qualities, namely, the acids and the tannins. That way, everything checks out.

SOME BASIC TERMS FOR ALCOHOL:
biting, blistering, brutal, burning, ferocious, fiery, heady, heated, hot, monstrous, nippy, potent, punchy, rasping, scorching, spirity, stingy, tingling, warming

ALCOHOL

Where does the alcohol come from? Answer: very ripe grapes have a high sugar content; when fermented, the sugar is converted to alcohol. Hot-weather climates produce riper grapes that have more sugar, which, in turn, produces more alcohol. Cool climates produce less ripe grapes, which, when fermented, produce lower-alcohol wines. Simple, yes?

Would you drink wine if it didn't have alcohol, such as those (awful) alcohol-free ersatz wines? Would you eat a meal without seasonings? I hope your answer is "Of course not."

One of the many pleasures of wine is its relatively modest alcohol content, which contributes to the enjoyment of meals with friends and family, with lovers, with business associates, with anyone who relishes good food, good wine, good company. Otherwise, what's the point?

Therefore, the point here is this: a little buzz from a good wine with good food is usually a pleasant experience if you can handle the alcohol. If you can't, stay away from wine and all other alcoholic beverages. You can live a long and happy life without ever drinking alcohol if you want to. (I, however, want to live a long and happy life with some wine every day with dinner.)

SOME ADVANCED LINGO FOR ALCOHOL:

anesthetizes my palate, burns on your tongue, head-spinning, towering inferno, fire-breathing level, don't light a match near here, high octane, tongue-nipping, viperous

THE BEAST WITHIN:

We humans are thought to have domesticated a dozen or so animals as early as about ten thousand years ago. We've lived with them ever since, these dogs, cats, cows, oxen, horses, chickens, ducks, geese, and other creatures that became our companions as well as our food sources. We know them well, their habits, particularly their smells. When we encounter certain aromas in wine, they may remind us of the animals that have been a part of our lives along the way.

Growing up, we may have had a pet beagle or enjoyed the neighbor's big friendly tail-wagger; some of us were lucky enough to have a horse or a pony. Others shared their formative years with a cat in the house.

Animal smells in wine bring all these memories back, no matter how long ago our relationships with these animals were. The mind almost never forgets a smell, for better or worse. This is why similar chemicals can and do produce the same perceptions and trigger these recollections.

Trust me here: there are no beasts lurking in your wineglass. No pets, no barnyard dwellers, no wild things. Now, aren't you relieved?

However, what if you still think that there's really something in the wine to wrinkle your nose at? Stay calm: it's only a slight alchemistic sleight of hand. *(Bow-wow, meow, moo, cluck, quack, oink!)*

SOME BASIC TERMS FOR ANIMAL:
camel, cat, chicken, cow, dog, duck, elephant, fish, fowl, fox, game, goat, horse, lamb, lion, monkey, mouse, pig, puppy, sheep, skunk, stallion, swan, worm

ANIMAL

Pee-yuu! This could mean something smells like an animal, even stinks. However, like so many sensory perceptions, a subtle touch can be nice; a lot, awful. It all depends on how animal smells affect you.

If you experience joy when you smell a freshly washed infant or mate (who are animals, after all), you're ready for a touch of animal in your wine. If you hate human or other animal smells, steer clear of aged red wines in particular; you'll probably hate them, too.

So where do these good/bad smells come from? The very same place all the others come from: the Earth and its biochemical tricksters. One of the biggest offenders is a chemical bad-boy called *brett*, short for *brettanomyces*, a nasty spoilage yeast that winemakers try to avoid at all cost. Brett is one stinker that makes wine smell like the wrong end of an animal. Run away.

Still, a slight touch of animal adds intrigue and complexity to wine. When you're ready for a bit of animal, look for red Burgundies and Rhônes, some of which are noted for, ahem, their barnyard characteristics.

Don't worry, though; there really aren't any dogs, cats, goats, jellyfish, or other varmints in your wine. I hope you knew that all along.

SOME ADVANCED LINGO FOR ANIMAL:

mashed ants, crushed bugs, cat-pee stinker, chicken guts, rotting fish, fowl droppings, randy goat, diabetic horse, manurey, dead mouse, resinous skunk

A FINE FIGURE:

Body is the heft of a wine, or the lack of it. It's a term for what you feel as the weight in your mouth. A popular analogy is to compare things like fat-free milk (light-bodied) to whole milk (medium-bodied), to heavy cream (full-bodied).

Uncomplicated young wines tend to be light; complex older wines tend to be heavy, particularly reds. Keep in mind that the word *body,* as I use it, is the sum total of all the tiny solids, sometimes called *extract*, another wine-trade term.

The concept of body, like effervescence, relates to tactile sensations inside your mouth, on your tongue, gums, and palate. You feel the weight of the wine, just as you feel the tickle of any bubbles and the cool refreshment of the liquid.

While the term *body* usually means weight in the mouth (often called *mouthfeel*), it can also mean aromas that nudge our memories into thinking about human bodies, or parts of human bodies—some we like to remember and some we don't. A lot of erotic images and memories abound here.

To most people, a nice body, a good body, is just that: attractive, balanced, poised, and memorable. A bad one is the opposite.

Don't make a big deal out of this, though, as you really aren't going to get a test at the end of the book.

SOME BASIC TERMS FOR BODY/VISCOSITY:

big, carnal, chewy, erotic, fat, fleshy, full, heavy, huge, lean, leggy, light, round, sensual, sexy, slippery, soft, syrupy, teary, thick, velvety, viscous, watery, weighty

BODY/VISCOSITY

All wine has viscosity but it's not motor oil (don't drink both to compare them).

Viscosity, sometimes known as *fluidity*, is what accounts for the, ahem, legs on the sides of a wineglass after swirling. These legs, or tears (boo-hoo), have no connection to quality; they only indicate a substantial level of alcohol.

A fine dessert wine may well be syrupy, especially if it's mature and/or expensive and rare. The renowned low-alcohol dessert wine called Château d'Yquem (dee-KEM), a French Sauternes, can be hideously expensive (over $1,000 a bottle). Yikes! After you taste a sip of this nectar, however, your *Yikes!* may well turn into a *Wow!*

Thin wine tastes thin because it has little body; fat wine tastes fat because it has many goodies in its makeup, all yammering for your mouth's attention. Still, don't get pushed into believing that thin wines are lousy. They're not. There are some wonderful thinner-style wines out there, particularly two French whites, Chablis and Muscadet, that have plenty of flavor, and they're both waiting for you to try them. They may have light bodies, but they can be wonderful when sipped alone or with light, summery food. It's all a matter of balance and appropriate matching to food.

Body and viscosity: two sides of the same concept. Find a body you like and follow your heart.

SOME ADVANCED LINGO FOR BODY/VISCOSITY:

ultrafull-bodied, what a body!, bosomy, seamless fleshpot, axle grease, lean and mean, oil slick, sensual? oh yes!, tears of joy, texture of 10W40 motor oil, almost weightless

DUST TO CANDY:

Have you ever been so thirsty you thought a hot, dry desert had formed in your mouth? Have you ever eaten or drunk something so gaggingly sweet that your face crinkled up in disgust? If so, you've already learned what dry and sweet are.

Dry tends to be a hard concept for new wine drinkers to master. *Dry* doesn't mean *not wet* in wine; it means only that there's no or just a touch of residual sugar in the wine. A good dry wine usually matches well with most food up to dessert; sweet wine goes best with (surprise!) sweet desserts.

Some people who dislike sweet wines call them *liquid candy.* Some people who hate dry wines describe them as *sand in the mouth.* At this stage of your wine education, it's important to learn that wines can have virtually no sweetness whatsoever (it's all been fermented out and converted into alcohol), while others have more sweetness than you or I could possibly imagine.

Good sweet wines are the ones made by real wine lovers who create their sweet wines knowing the wines must be balanced with enough acid to counteract the sweetness. Not all winemakers tend to acknowledge this, which is the reason some sweet wines are unbalanced.

If you prefer dry, stay with it. If you like sweet, drink sweet and enjoy it.

SOME BASIC TERMS FOR DRY TO SWEET:
arid, bittersweet, *brut*, cloying, dryish, nonsweet, oversugared, oversweet, semidry, semisweet, sticky, sugary, sweet, sweetened, sweetie, sweetish, ultradry, ultrasweet

DRY TO SWEET

Sweetness in wine is easy to detect, hard to explain. Almost all red table wines (wines to drink with food) have virtually no sugar left in them after fermentation (meaning no residual sugar). Many whites, however, do have varying levels of sugar that was never fermented into alcohol. To many wine aficionados who love their vino dry, that is, wine with no perceptible sweetness, the worst possible liquid to put into a glass is a sweet wine. The reverse holds true for sweet-wine lovers.

Dry wines go best with food, particularly appetizers and entrées. Sweet wines usually accompany desserts if they're sweet.

There are carloads of cheap, ghastly sweet wines out there that have discouraged many a casual wine drinker from enjoying a high-quality sweet dessert wine, let alone a dry wine to go with meals. Avoid these bottles of low-end sweet wines; they'll probably offer you no satisfaction.

However, and it's a big however, there's a definite place for sweet wines at the end of a meal. These can be a gorgeous Sauternes from France, a sprightly Moscato d'Asti from Italy, a luscious late-harvest ice wine from Germany or Canada, or even a rare and rich Tokaji wine from Hungary. The people who drink these perfectly balanced sweet wines call them heaven in a glass.

SOME ADVANCED LINGO FOR DRY TO SWEET:

ashes in the throat, as cloying as candy, dental nightmare, blisteringly dry, sickly sugary glop, flabby sugar bomb, sugarcanelike, smells sweet, powder-keg dry, electric sweetness

---

THE DIRT UNDER OUR FEET:

The Earth as we know it is the only one we have, or will probably ever have. We stand and run on it every day of our lives, and beneath our feet is earth (small e)—the dirt, the soil, the land, the stuff that grows things. Like grapes that make wine. Since these very same grapes draw their nourishment from this very same earth, they always mirror the chemistry and biology of that soil. And the air and the weather around them (some folks call this *terroir;* see page 10).

We humans have only been around a few million years, a blink in geologic time. Still, we've all experienced what the Earth is, how it smells at different times, and what its products are like.

Just look at the list at the bottom to get a tiny introduction to the many qualities you could find in wine, from grass to gravel, from ferns to forest, from smoke to sun, from water to woods.

Wine has the strongest possible affinity to this Earth, from its origins as a grapevine that produces the grapes that we convert into wine. Neat, eh?

Some wines seem to reflect many of the local characteristics of the areas where their grapes grow, even producing salty or saline sensations because the vineyard is near the ocean, with its sea breezes and foamy sprays. With all that salt air around, some of it just has to get reflected in the wine. Beach wine, anyone?

SOME BASIC TERMS FOR EARTH:
air, breeze, chalk, clay, compost, dirt, grass, gravel, hay, lawn, leaf, mineral, moss, mulch, peat, pebbles, quartz, rock, slate, soil, stone, swampy, volcano, water, weed

EARTH

Have you ever been out hiking and stopped at a mountain stream to drink the fresh, pure water? And possibly put a smooth wet stone in your mouth to suck on? Both of those are the taste of the Earth, along with lots of others—outdoorsy stuff like forest floors, leaf litter, wild herbs, mushroomy things, trees and bushes, wild vines, and many, many others.

Different grapes like different soils to grow in. Some need more or fewer minerals, some more or less rain, drainage, sunshine, altitude, fertilizer, pesticides, whatever. Just like people, who each have different needs beyond the basics.

Wine is a great conjurer. It pulls many of these mimicking organics right out of the soil. And gives itself the blessing of the Earth it came from.

The sky above, the mud below, fresh air and foul, rich compost and dead sand, everything and anything that could and would grow is there in your glass, whether you like it or not.

Red wines generally carry more of what we call the earthy qualities; in whites, they tend to be harder to detect.

Nonetheless, if you love the smell of fresh-mown grass, warm hay, salt air, hot sand, and many others, you'll also love the aromas that wine can produce. Few other products of nature can offer such gifts.

SOME ADVANCED LINGO FOR EARTH:

volcanic ash, plain ol' dirt, earthy perfume, rain forest, mineral pit, wet ground moss, river rocks, wet slate, freshly tilled soil, rotting straw, stagnant pond water

IN FULL BLOOM:

There are all kinds of flower scents in wine, which isn't so far-fetched when you realize that wine is made from grapes that grow on vines that the bees have to pollinate so that the flowers could turn into the fruit that ripens into what we call *grapes*. Clever, eh?

Flowers are everywhere in our lives. Every city has flower markets, gardens and parks, window boxes and pots. Many of us visit botanical gardens, conservatories, and city parks. We live in a world surrounded by flowers.

Wine, the great chameleon of liquids, puts forth many illusions that flowers were dragged through it. Not true. There are no flowers in wine, just the same chemical molecules that give flowers their characteristic scents. The grapevines have extracted all manner of chemicals and minerals from the ground, and these are the culprits. We believe we can smell everything in the list below, and we can, in a manner of speaking.

Some wine drinkers love the smell of flowers in their gardens; on their decks, tables, and porches; and in their wines. If they do, they should seek out those wines that emit strong floral scents. A good example is an aromatic wine called Gewürztraminer; another is Muscat. Think of them as floral arrangements in your wineglass.

SOME BASIC TERMS FOR FLOWERS:

daffodils, elderflowers, fresh, geraniums, heather, honeysuckle, lavender, lilacs, lilies, marigolds, orchids, peonies, roses, tulips, violets, wildflowers, wisteria, zinnias

FLOWERS

A floral wine is generally a young and fruity wine (there are exceptions like the Italian Barolos, which have been described as having the aromas of both tar and roses). Say what? What is a wine that smells of lavender, of fresh rose petals, of dying tulips? So much of the aroma of wine begins and ends with floral notes that we often label wines as *floral*. And why not?

Is there the scent of a flower on earth that someone hasn't sniffed in wine? Unlikely, since floral wines, and all wines, for that matter, come from grapes, and grapes come from flowers. But you just learned that.

One of the ways you can improve your perception of the floral quality of wine is to visit flower markets and smell deeply of the many kinds and types of flowers. If you have a garden, or live near a park with flowers, do the same there. You'd be surprised how many new nuances of *floral* you'll be able to pick out in wine.

Still, wine drinkers love to go on and on about this floral quality or that floral quality. So utterly b-o-r-i-n-g. In this case, you've probably heard of someone called a *wine bore,* someone who's in love with his or her own voice and just can't help but tell anyone who'll listen about all the wonderful qualities perceived in this glass, including floral notes. Run away.

SOME ADVANCED LINGO FOR FLOWERS:

Easter basket, Edenic bouquet, carpet of daffodils, lavender in bloom, roasted lilacs, nectar-dripping orchids, crushed roses, marsh marigolds, faded tulips, bitter violets

YOU ARE WHAT YOU EAT:

This is a huge category of wine expressions, as our memory banks are packed with sensations of just about everything we have ever smelled or tasted before. We're human, and we never forget what went into our noses and mouths, an entire life's worth of diet, soup to nuts, as it were.

Every wine-tasting term related to food conjures up not only the aromas and flavors and textures of food, but the *where* and *when*. Food is as much context as content. We are very much what we eat—good food or bad, tasty or lousy, spicy or bland, sweet or bitter.

Fruit: if there's one characteristic of wine that shines brightly above many others, it has to be fruit. Wine is born of ripe grapes and tells our mouths right away where it comes from.

Ooh, veggies! As kids, with some exceptions (you know who you are), we hated eating most vegetables. However, we're grown up now, and we not only drink wine but also eat veggies—lots and lots of veggies.

We also love a good deal of seasonings if that's the way we were brought up: spice it up here, hot sauce it there, slather it with condiments that could ignite a campfire.

The category of *food* presents a dizzying array of smells and tastes that conjure up countless sensory collections. Enjoy all these memories of your lifetime.

SOME BASIC TERMS FOR FOOD, INCLUDING FRUITS, VEGETABLES, HERBS, SPICES, NUTS, AND BEVERAGES:

apples, bacon, basil, beans, bread, butter, cake, candy, cheese, coffee, cookies, cream, eggs, honey, jam, meat, milk, peaches, pepper, salt, soda, tea, toast, vanilla, walnuts

FOOD, INCLUDING FRUITS, VEGETABLES, HERBS, SPICES, NUTS, AND BEVERAGES

We never seem to forget the tastes from childhood: warm chocolate cookies, cold sweet milk, fresh cinnamon doughnuts, apple pie, strawberry ice cream, hot dogs, candy bars, jelly beans. We hold on to the past, whether we like to or not.

Many young wines are so fruity that many people call them *fruit bombs*. Sure, wine comes from fruit, but it doesn't always have to replicate the fruit stall every time you swallow.

Vegetables are another matter entirely. Like it or not, many wines conjure up mental images of all the veggies we ever ate, from mushrooms to peas.

Another trait unique to us humans: we just love to season our food, a little or a lot. With delicate herbs, not-so-subtle spices, even nuts.

Wines can be fruity, vegetal, mild, strong, bland, spicy, or nutty. They mimic all the things that we have ever eaten or drunk since our births.

The magic of wine is the magic of pleasure and pain, of good times and bad, of people you want to remember and people you don't, of those special moments that have made your life unique and interesting. Enjoy every sensation wine can offer you. After all, that's why you drink it, right?

SOME ADVANCED LINGO FOR FOOD, INCLUDING FRUITS, VEGETABLES, HERBS, SPICES, NUTS, AND BEVERAGES:

barnyard asparagus, smoky bacon fat, rancid fairy cake, peanut butter, burnt cabbage, fish oil, rotten garlic, hater-ade, V-8® juice, sour milk, funky nuts, ghastly pickle juice, Devil Dogs®

DON'T FORGET THE GLORY:

There are wines so light and delicate you can barely taste them. There are wines so powerful they almost knock you off your chair. What an amazing liquid!

The problem for many wine drinkers is that they don't really understand what level of power they like in a wine. They'll drink something delicate with a steak or roast, or something strong with fish or vegetable hors d'oeuvres. Major mistake. Powerful wines need powerful food to accompany them; delicate wines need delicate food.

If you like hardy, go for a big red, such as a Cabernet Sauvignon or an Argentine Malbec. If you like delicate, ask for a crisp, dry white like an unoaked Chardonnay or a dry Riesling. That way you'll find the perfect accompaniment.

A powerful wine doesn't caress your nose and palate; it confronts them. It tells you to sit up and take notice because it has something to say. It has *extract*, the sum total of all the solids in wine. Powerful wines, particularly reds with lots of tannin, will usually provide you with a memorable mouthful. Don't shy away; this could be an important lesson in wine knowledge: the more you taste, the more you learn; the more you learn, the better the wine will taste. Simple.

Wine has other powers, one of which is to remind us to relive certain experiences from the past.

SOME BASIC TERMS FOR POWER:

assertive, bruiser, concentrated, delicate, dense, extracted, energetic, explosive, feisty, fierce, forceful, gentle, gutsy, intense, punchy, staining, strong, virile, weak, wimpy

POWER

Watch out, though, because powerful wines usually have high, or at least higher, alcohol content that should be factored in when drinking. After you've finished a bottle of a high-alcohol red, remember not to take to the road.

Also, note that power doesn't equal quality—at least not usually. There are many wine drinkers who prefer subtlety over power. If you're one, focus on the fact that you're pleasing yourself—no one else—and enjoy all the nuances that a good wine, a fine wine, can offer you.

On the other hand, or tongue, do try some of the blisteringly strong wines available. You may not want to drink them every day, but remember them when you're facing a winter dinner of roast meat, steak or chops, big stews, or other heavy foods. Rich food needs rich wines, and rich wines, with plenty of body, tannin, alcohol, and fruit, are the perfect companions.

These wines also usually have long finishes that go on and on long after you swallow. If that's something that appeals to you, by all means go for it.

Wine is all about pleasure, yours especially, and that of your dining partner(s) as well. Make every meal with someone you care about memorable. File every wine you drink away in your memory for retrieval at just the right moment.

SOME ADVANCED LINGO FOR POWER:
velvety bombshell, fist-in-the-face, feral intensity, Mighty Mouse®, pistol-packing, revved-up powerhouse, sense of shock and awe, slap upside your head, pumps iron

ARCHITECTURAL DETAILS:

When you build a house, you build it to stay up, good weather or bad, calm days or windy, dry nights or wet.

Wine has similar needs: it has to be strong enough to weather the time in the barrel or bottle, the time and movement of shipping, the temperature and humidity of wherever it is. In other words, wine needs a sound structure to last long enough to get sipped and poured down your parched throat.

Wine *structure* is an elusive term. It's hard to describe and measure. If you tell people that the wine they're drinking has a sturdy structure that'll help the wine age, don't be surprised if your companions look at you strangely. Just tell them that structure is what holds the wine together and gives it definition.

The best way to describe wine structure is to say that the fruit, the sugars, the acidity, the tannin, and the body are all there, supporting each other and providing a sound architecture (structure) for the wine to live out its life, short or long.

We humans have structure just like wine: we have spines and we have backbones. Wine, too. Those very same things hold us all up, and supply us, like wine, with shape and definition. We are all precisely framed—a good thing for us and wine.

SOME BASIC TERMS FOR STRUCTURE:

asymmetrical, backbone, bones, formless,
big-framed, small-framed, framework,
platform, scaffolding, scale, skeleton,
spineless, structured, top-heavy

STRUCTURE

Usually, few of us, if any, spend a lot of time thinking about the structure of a wine, unless that wine's basics—acid, body, fruit, sugar, and tannin—are badly out of whack. This elusive concept tends to puzzle wine drinkers because there's no easy handle on it to grasp: should we say this wine has good structure or bad structure or no structure at all? Does it have good bones, a flexible but sturdy spine, a solid foundation that will endure over time? Should we even pay attention to anyone talking about structure as if it were a do-or-die quality? Perhaps; perhaps not.

Wine can't fall down like a house on a poor foundation, but a wine with poor structure sure can put a damper on enjoyment without your even being aware of it. In fact, you could go through your whole life enjoying wine without having the slightest idea what wine structure involves.

Just drink the stuff . . . your handsome nose and beautiful mouth will tell you in short order whether the wine is up to snuff, whether it has all the right stuff in all the right places. If you say, *mmm,* after a sip, or *phooey,* after a sip, that's really pretty much it with respect to structure. Just keep on sipping and hoping you get far more of those tasty *mmms. Yum* is good, too.

SOME ADVANCED LINGO FOR STRUCTURE:
architecturally perfect, more backbone than
a humpback whale, rack of bones, sinewy
framework, dependable platform, built like
a brick you-know-what house

PUCKER UP:

You've heard of tanned leather? Then you've heard of tannin, which is what's used to tan (ahem) leather. It's also found in wine, mostly red wine, and comes from the grape skins and stems of red grapes. It's what gives red wines their puckeriness and gives most red wine its longevity, because it's a natural preservative. But don't just drink tannin alone in order to live to 150; your digestive system can't take it.

Tannin is the component that supplies wine its astringent quality, so fancied by wine connoisseurs and everyday drinkers like me. I love that little bit of pucker that pokes around in my mouth, saying, "Hi, I'm a nice red wine with just a little bite to let you know I'm here. Like to taste some more of me?" Some people, however, don't care for that tactile quality, which is why they prefer white wine that doesn't have much tannin. Much smoother and usually easier to drink, think they.

Nevertheless, take a look at the wine terms at the bottom of this page for some other descriptors of tannin, and see if you'd like some of those very qualities. If you do, drink reds; if you don't, drink whites or rosés. No one will come and arrest me for telling you all this or arrest you for drinking what you like (at least I hope not).

SOME BASIC TERMS FOR TANNIN:
abrasive, aggressive, assertive, astringent, biting, bitter, blistering, gravelly, green, grippy, gritty, hard, jagged, melting, painful, puckery, raspy, ripe, rough, smooth, viperous

TANNIN

One quotation about tannin I remember is this: "If you like chewing on an old leather belt or bedroom slipper, you'll love wine with lots of tannin." Oh, really? Maybe I'm strange, but I don't like chewing on stuff like that. A little tannin or a bit of pucker goes a long way.

On the other hand, many of the health benefits of wine come from tannin, because it's a natural preservative as well as an antioxidant. Drink a moderate amount of red wine every day and you may be able to fight off some of life's truly ghastly diseases or other afflictions.

Tannin, along with acid, alcohol, fruit, and sugar, is one of the essentials in wine. A little tannin in balance is a very good thing; a lot of tannin isn't, and makes the wine unbalanced. Try enough red wines, such as the low-tannin Beaujolais, Dolcetto, or Pinot Noir during this learning curve on wine.

By the way, there's a grape out there in France called *tannat,* which makes a fiercely powerful wine in Gascony's Madiran region. When you come across it, try a little and learn what the word *tan* really means. If you drink a lot of this, I wonder if your lips will get tanned into leather. . . . just kidding.

SOME ADVANCED LINGO FOR TANNIN:
biting asperity, dusty astringency, piercing daggers, impenetrable, scabrous, tannic bra, cast-iron tannins, no hard vulgar tannins, undrinkably tough, sweaty . . . leathery

AT THE LUMBERYARD:

It's a good thing we're not termites; they must just hate unoaked wine. No cellulose, no sap, no splinters. But there are some wine drinkers who love the aroma and taste of wood in their wine. These could well be the legions of California Chardonnay lovers who can't or won't drink anything else. You'd think their mothers were beavers the way they gobble up the heavily oaked Chard. Guess it's a trees-for-the-forest thing.

The actual culprit is an organic compound called *aldehyde* that seeps into the wine during fermentation. Consequently, there's no real wood lurking in wine; only the perceived aroma and taste of oak, especially American oak, which has a powerfully woody character (French oak, much more expensive than American oak, is finer-grained and milder). If you want to see a major food fight—make that a wine fight—just listen to how wood lovers and wood haters carry on. You'd think someone insulted their family or called their children ugly. You know better, since you're starting to develop your own taste sense.

Wood is good for houses and furniture; it's also good in wine, if used carefully with restraint. Moderate aging in wood barrels can and usually does give wine extra dimension and character. Beware, however, of the cheaper wines that assume people are distantly related to termites.

SOME BASIC TERMS FOR WOOD:
balsam, bark, cedar, maple, oak, oaked, oaky, pine, redwood, sap, sawdust, splintery, timber, tree, twig, unoaked, unwooded, vanilla, willow, woody, yew

WOOD

You should be aware that not all winemakers use wood responsibly. Some vintners, more like bulk wine manufacturers, try to keep their prices low, so they often don't even use real oak barrels; instead, they use cheaper oak chips, or even oak sawdust in giant teabags that soak in the wine to give it instant aging. Yuck! Double yuck!

No good wine, no great wine, is ever overoaked so you'd notice the aroma or taste of wood. Keep that in mind when drinking whites, especially heavily wooded ones from the New World.

Another nail in the (wood) wine coffin: if you love the taste of fresh, the kind of fresh that's often associated with good whites that are food-friendly, know that most, if not all, are unwooded. That way, they're swell with all kinds of dishes and they make memorable food partners at a fine meal, especially seafood.

Don't get yourself crazed over the wood content of wine. By the time you finish this book, you will have tried many different wines, some with no wood, some with a little, some with a lot. You're all grown up; make your own choices.

To summarize: unless you're descended from termites or beavers, you ought not to have a strong love affair with woody wines. A little goes a long way; a lot may give you splinters in your mouth. Ouch, that hurts!

SOME ADVANCED LINGO FOR WOOD:
gnarly cedar, burnt firewood, oaky monster, bubble-gum oak, liquid oak, termite's fantasy dinner, splintered two-by-four, wooden bra, woodpecker heaven

THE NOSE KNOWS:

*T*here are more things in heaven and earth . . . No one said it better than Shakespeare's Hamlet. And he was right on when it comes to talking about wine, since we find just about everything in it, sometimes even the proverbial kitchen sink (someone once described a wine as smelling like a kitchen drain). Ugh.

If you want to give your smelling and tasting apparatus a good run for the money, get your hands on some complex red wines, such as Cabernet Sauvignon or Pinot Noir with a bit of age on them; clear your mind, pay no attention to anything around you, close your eyes, and just smell, smell, smell and sip, sip, sip. Maybe you'll be spared detecting unclean kitchen drains, but you could smell some favorite old leather boots, horse blankets, railroad stations, fish nets, Band-Aids®, your lover's skin, your mother's cologne, your grandmother's cookies, your childhood pet dog, rubber gloves. All these aromas and tastes—and thousands more—can and do pop up in wine.

Wine can and will conjure up the most unlikely and unexpected perceptions imaginable. Go with it; it's one of the most interesting facets of wine. The more wines you smell and taste, the more impressions you'll have; some nice, some much less so. Sort of like people: we like some, not others. Not so strange, eh?

SOME BASIC TERMS FOR OTHER AROMAS, OTHER TASTES:

asphalt, cage, cellar, funk, gas, glue, leather, matchstick, mouthwash, oil, paint, paper, pencil, petrol, polish, powder, saddle, sheet, shop, smoke, soap, socks, stable, tar, wax

---

OTHER AROMAS, OTHER TASTES

Being a shape-shifting chameleon of smells and tastes, wine can leave you breathless with its ability to play with your head. Not to mention the many memories inside it.

This is, by far, the wackiest category of wine appreciation. Nobody could make up these wine descriptors. Still, people do detect them, or think they do.

There's no single liquid other than wine that could possibly conjure up so many weird descriptions of what wine drinkers detect. Aren't you glad you'll only come across very few of them? I know I am. Very glad.

While we all have the same systems for smelling and tasting that have evolved over millions of years to protect us from swallowing bad things, each of us has a unique sensory profile shared by no other nose or mouth in the universe. We are very much what we smell, what we taste, eat, or drink. In plain language, we are human.

Supersmellers and supertasters, that is, people at the high end of the sensitivity scale, detect many more qualities than most of us do. A touch of salt to them screams *salty*! A little oak roars *woody*! To these people, it's called the curse of supersensitivity.

Still, when it comes to describing weird things we smell or taste in wine, the sky's the limit for most of us. As it should be.

**SOME ADVANCED LINGO FOR
OTHER AROMAS, OTHER TASTES:**

bad car accident on a hot day, moldy Band-Aids®,
wet horse blanket, hamster cage, condom
powder, diesel exhaust, Liquid Draño®,
Lemon Pledge®, sewer gas, old lady perfume

HIGH-WIRE ACT:

Have you ever walked on something really narrow, like a board, a wall, a fence, or a balance beam, and suddenly knew how hard it was to do without falling off? That's balance at work.

Balance is also hard to achieve in wine. So many things can go wrong, and frequently do: too much of this, too little of that. It's very hard to get it right, which is the reason only the better, and best, wines have fine balance. Most cheapies don't. Don't even bother looking for decent balance in wines costing $10 or less. There usually isn't any.

So what should you expect when searching for balance in a wine? Acid, sugar, fruit, tannin, body, and alcohol—all should be in harmony so that what you perceive is the perfect combination of components. Nothing is lacking; nothing stands out.

Not so easy to achieve, however. You've heard of the fruit bomb: all fruit, all the time. You've heard about 18 percent alcohol levels; one drink and you're almost under the table. Tannins so powerful they'll pucker your mouth to a whimper. Acids so strong they'll scour your mouth clean for days. Sugar enough to gag on. And too heavy a body for a delicate ballerina.

Get the picture? Not a pretty sight, is it? Neither is an unbalanced wine.

SOME BASIC TERMS FOR BALANCE:
centered, cohesive, disjointed, equilibrium, harmonious, harmony, integrated, orderly, proportioned, seamless, symmetrical, together, unbalanced, ungainly, unstable

BALANCE

How on earth do you find wines with good balance? One way that works: ask a knowledgeable wine store employee or an experienced wine server in a restaurant. These people have tasted hundreds, perhaps thousands, of wines; they know very well which wines are balanced and which aren't. Trust their expertise until your knowledge grows to where you're comfortable making your own personal judgments.

Balance is one of the hardest wine concepts to grasp because it's so subtle. However, be persistent; the more you taste the more you'll learn. At some point, you'll be able to distinguish the good balance of a fine wine from the unbalanced ordinary. When you taste a new or unfamiliar wine, listen to your nose and mouth; they'll tell you soon enough whether the fruit is too forward, the acids too cutting, the alcohol too hot, the tannins too biting, the wood too dominant.

Think of balance as harmony. A well-made wine has a harmony of aroma and taste tones similar to the music played by a fine orchestra. You know it when you hear it. In wine, you know it when you smell and taste it.

Balance in wine is sometimes difficult to perceive. If all else fails, try the test of absence and presence: a well-balanced wine gives you nothing to criticize; an unbalanced one does.

SOME ADVANCED LINGO FOR BALANCE:
well-composed, impeccable equilibrium, smartly integrated, not a hair out of place, utterly seamless, hauntingly symmetrical, out of kilter, tightrope walker, out of whack

NO SIMPLE SIMON:

The basic wine quenches your thirst, washes your food down, and can give you a buzz if you drink enough of it. It doesn't have any dimensions, or layers, or enough of various qualities to distinguish it. It's simply, well, simple.

Complex wines, however, are a whole different story. They can change from minute to minute after being poured; they can present different layers of aroma and taste as they warm up or cool down; they can get you thinking about all the different character-istics that you recognize. In other words, these wines have what wine lovers call *complexity.* Not unlike a problem, a poem, a book, or a play. Layers upon layers, in other words.

Just don't expect much, if any, complexity in cheap, basic, everyday wines. Their purpose is to slake thirst, rather than thrill your nose and mouth in the process of partnering with fine food. Do expect, however, some complexity in better wines; for example, artisanal wines that have been produced carefully, with skill and love, the kind of wines we would always want to drink if we could afford them (or if we can convince someone else to buy them to share). With more experience drinking many different wines, you'll be able to detect more complexity.

SOME BASIC TERMS FOR COMPLEXITY:
deep, delineated, depth, focused, integrated, intricate, monothematic, multidimensional, multilayered, nuanced, orchestrated, precise, simple, spectrum, uncomplicated

COMPLEXITY

Try to imagine, if you can, an orchestra or band playing only two instruments: one plays the high notes and one plays the low notes. Sounds pretty boring, right? The same with wine; sure, it can slake your thirst or lubricate your throat, but it may not have many layers of aroma and taste, considerable depth or dimensions to keep you enthralled.

But a big orchestra, with many instruments playing in harmony, or a rock band with a dozen well-amplified performers all doing their things together, can thrill with everything going on. That's complexity.

Wine is the same: it, too, has high notes and low; it has hard tones and soft; it has fruity qualities, acidic sharpness, mellow tannins, balanced sugars, and velvety contours. That's complexity.

When you drink a fine wine, pay close attention to all the aspects of it as it rolls around in your mouth before swallowing. You should be able to pick out three, four, or even five different qualities—the mark of a good effort in the winery by people who care about the wine they make and bottle.

Complexity is a hard concept for new wine drinkers to comprehend. Give yourself some time and exposure to different wines to get the hang of it.

**SOME ADVANCED LINGO
FOR COMPLEXITY:**

deftly amalgamated, lots of bandwidth, as deep as a mineshaft, bottomless depth of flavors, ferocious focus, layers and layers, symphony of sensations

ACCORDING TO TYPE:

The one sure thing about wine is that there's no such thing as a typical wine in the abstract. Wines that are called typical are typical only of their origin, their grapes, or their vintage (the year the grapes were harvested and/or when the wine was made). Wines that demonstrate *typicality* (sometimes called *typicity*) are considered to be of better quality than wines that could come from anywhere, without any specific background. Don't be confused here; *typicality* isn't a snobby word meant to trick you. Simply believe that most good wines should taste like they come from particular places and are made from particular grapes by particular people.

One of the key concepts inherent in typicality is whether or not the wine demonstrates the classic qualities of the grapes that made it. Does this taste the way a buttery Chardonnay should? Does this taste like an earthy Pinot Noir? If they do, they're typical. Otherwise, they're not.

The same with grapes. Zinfandel grapes shouldn't taste like Merlot grapes, nor should Sauvignon Blanc grapes taste like Riesling grapes. A wine made in the south of France shouldn't taste like a wine made in the south of Australia. A wine made in cool Germany shouldn't taste like a wine made in cool Oregon. In other words, each according to its origin and heritage.

SOME BASIC TERMS FOR TYPICALITY/TYPICITY:

atypical, blend, characteristic, classic, crossover, curiosity, idiosyncratic, modern, New World, Old World, regional, representative, rustic, sipper, unlikely, throwback, unusual, varietal

TYPICALITY/TYPICITY

Yes, this is another hard concept to get right.
Wine pros, Old-World or New-, at least agree
that this characteristic of wine reflects a wine's
birthplace and origin, similar to the even more complicated concept of *terroir*.

Wines that are typical of their origins or regions all
show common properties that are recognizable, at
least to the pros. For those of you still mastering the
basics of wine, appreciate what a typical California
Zinfandel is, or an Italian Chianti, or an Australian
Riesling. More, a French Burgundy, an Alsatian Pinot
Gris, an Argentine Malbec or a New Zealand Sauvignon
Blanc. If you can master this lesson, you're on the way
to achieving wine knowledge from A to Z.

Typicality is just a fancy word for where the wine
came from, what style or type it is, what kind of
grapes were used, even, is it made from a single grape
or a vineyard, or a blend?

Don't get hung up on the subtle concept of typicality.
Leave it to the pros to haggle over. Your job, should you
accept it, is to drink as many wines as you can, and to
become more familiar with all the vino out there. After
all, the point of this very book is to get your nose
sniffing, your mouth sipping, and your throat swallowing all kinds of different wines to find just the right
ones for you. A pleasant form of education, is it not?

SOME ADVANCED LINGO FOR
TYPICALITY/TYPICITY:

back-to-basics approach, bastard child, bogus
blend, neither fish nor fowl, Frankenwine, red
painted black, bog-standard rosé, take-no-
prisoners-style, *vino crudo*, wine lite

THE CHECKERED FLAG:

Speaking of the checkered flag, we're almost but not quite at the end. The word *finish* in the context of wine usually means one thing: how long did the flavor seem to last when you finally swallowed it? Barely any time at all? Not so good. A while? Much better. A long, long time? Great!

One of the best quotes on *finish* came from the great wine expert Maynard A. Amerine, the late professor of enology at the University of California at Davis. He wrote: "The fine wine leaves you with something pleasant; the ordinary wine just leaves."

As a beginning wine drinker, don't get too bogged down as to whether the wine you're drinking has a long finish, say, a half-minute or even more that you can still feel in your throat after swallowing. All wines have a finish, aftertaste, or persistence. Except for water, most liquids do. In the case of a good wine, that aftertaste should, at the very least, be pleasant.

As you become more proficient in tasting wine, try to follow closely what happens when you swallow it. The reason we sip wine rather than swill it down is to savor all the obvious as well as subtle sensations our lips, mouth, tongue, and throat feel. That's what wine tasting is about.

SOME BASIC TERMS FOR FINISH:
acidic, aftertaste, bitter, chocolate, clean, clipped, crispy, dry, earthy, fruity, hot, lemon, lingering, long, minerally, minty, oak, prolonged, persistent, short, sweet, tannic, vanilla, woody

FINISH

When the wine you're drinking finally slips down your throat after being encouraged to slide around your mouth and tongue, you're at the finish line. A memorable finish is usually, some say always, the mark of a superior wine that's been made with fabulous grapes, great attention to detail, and love—a wine to savor and respect.

There aren't many wine experts who agree on just how a wine gets a long finish. Some say the soil, some say the grapes, some say the vinification process, and some say the aging. Whatever the case, don't get too frustrated trying to understand exactly why Wine A lasts just seventeen seconds and why Wine B lasts forty-two seconds. Just enjoy the sensation and go for another sip. It's a great way to appreciate a fine wine whenever and wherever you find it.

Another observation: some experts proclaim that a long finish is a characteristic of fine wines only. Possibly. More likely it's just one indicator, not an absolute confirmation.

Finally, here at the finish line, we can say just one thing: no one can predict accurately whether a wine will have a long finish or not. One thing is clear, however: you really should try a lot of different wines to find the answer to this problem. That shouldn't present a problem, should it?

SOME ADVANCED LINGO FOR FINISH:
curt aftertaste, shaft of bitterness, cymbal-crashing, enduring and heavenly, long sultry finish, lasts all night, lethally long, palate-staining, woody-rough, voluptuous

YUM, YUCK, OR SO-SO:

Being human, we all want to get to *yum.* And avoid *yuck,* if at all possible. One of the challenges of wine is that until we pull the cork or unscrew the cap on some unfamiliar bottle, we never know what we're going to find. That's the whole reason behind the adventure and excitement of wine tasting: to see if the stuff inside is good or not so good. That's the very definition of a wine lover: always searching for that memorable new wine experience. It's similar to the reason gamblers go to casinos: the next big score.

Much of what we describe as *quality* is really the sum total of the entire drinking/dining experience. A frosty glass of Chablis to go with perfectly fresh French *Belon* oysters, served on a beautiful flower-scented terrace overlooking the azure Mediterranean with your beloved at your side. This has to be one of the greatest sensory pleasures any human can have. You'll certainly remember that magic experience decades later.

How do you find out what's a good wine? Practice, practice, practice. And learn, learn, learn about balance, complexity, finish.

Evaluating wine quality is not all that difficult. Like what you like; if it tastes good to you, you probably have a good glass of wine. If not, keep looking and tasting.

SOME BASIC TERMS FOR QUALITY:

aromatic, bad, charming, classy, decadent, delicious, depraved, elegant, flashy, good, graceful, great, joyous, magical, mind-boggling, opulent, perfect, plonky, rich, subtle, swill, underwhelming

QUALITY

I s there a recommended wine you like, or is there a recommended wine you don't like? This conundrum has puzzled wine drinkers since we began to drink fermented fruit juice thousands of years ago. Is taste really in the eyes/nose/mouth of the beholder? Is there such a thing as objective *quality*? Of course, you already know the answer: yes and no. Now, aren't you relieved?

This is the final chapter on wine appreciation. By now, you should have picked up all kinds of pointers showing you the way to gaining wine knowledge. In addition, that wisdom, in a nutshell, should last you your whole life long, especially when you find a wine you like, or, better still, a fabulous wine you absolutely love.

I personally believe that a good wine is the wine you like, fine quality or less so. I also believe that, with practice and experience, you can learn to distinguish between a fine wine and an everyday wine. For example, after you drink some of your Uncle Mario's latest homemade plonk, er, wine, try, if you can, to get a taste of a Domaine Serene 2007 Pinot Noir from Oregon, a Rodney Strong 2007 Chardonnay from California, or a Louis Roederer Brut Champagne NV (nonvintage) from France. If you notice a significant difference, and you should by now, then you've figured out what this book is all about.

SOME ADVANCED LINGO FOR QUALITY:
bloody beautiful, wickedly delicious, truly disgusting, total dreck, brutally good, mind-boggling, rock-bottom plonk, stinky rotten wine, verges on the sublime, godawful

PART

3

*She poured the thick rubylike liquid,
and a seductive cloud of perfumes
swirled and filled the air. It reminded me
of fragrances of tropical fruit in Burma,
spices from the market in Marrakech,
cinnamon from the high valleys of the
Seychelles, the scent after a downpour
in the Marquesas, singly and together,
like banked clouds before a storm.
We drank without a word.*

—Ferenc Máté

WINE AND HEALTH

Did you know that drinking red wine regularly but moderately could be healthy for you? Are you aware that red wine has all kinds of beneficial ingredients to help your body fight off the nasties that attack it? No? Read on.

Study after study has shown that red wine, yes, the red wine we can and do drink every day, contains chemical substances that fight oxidants (bad for people) with antioxidants (good for people); one well-known disease-fighting component is called *resveratrol*. Resveratrol is so potent that drug companies are now putting it in pill form to take every morning along with vitamins (thanks, but I'll keep taking my resveratrol in liquid form, if you don't mind).

So where does this health benefit come from? The same place the red color comes from: the grape skins, which are packed with microchemical pigments for color as well as tannins for preservation, some beneficial acids, and the resveratrol that offer humans a chance to help battle cancers and other medical insults.

Wine has been acknowledged for millennia to be good for humans if drunk in moderation. Red wine drinkers who take some every day with their meals live longer than people who don't, although some people dispute this (not I, however).

Without delving into all the scientific gobbledygook, drinking red wine both tastes good, usually, and is also good for you, usually. Now go forth and consume that wine, but responsibly. In addition, don't forget to smile while you swallow this very tasty medicine, as in, open wide and say *aaah*.

WHAT TO DRINK WHEN

People who visit wineries sometimes get the chance to taste wines at the end of the manufacturing process; the wines are about as young as possible, often just barely drinkable. Because wine is a living liquid, always changing, always growing and aging, we've come to realize that wine usually needs a bit of time in the bottle to rest and gather itself together to mellow out.

Usually but not always. The media hysteria over the annual November release of French Beaujolais Nouveau is an example: this infantile red has hardly finished bubbling in the fermentation tank when it's bottled at high speed and rushed to stores worldwide in a marketing frenzy, presumably because the Beaujolais wine trade wants to convince people that drinking the youngest wine available is almost like eating the ripe grapes right off the vine. On the downside, Beaujolais Nouveau is usually dead within a year of bottling—talk about a short life span!

Almost all whites age faster than reds, and usually should be consumed sooner rather than later. Reds, which have more natural tannins as preservatives, can and do age for longer periods, sometimes for decades, a few even for a century or more (like us).

There are also beautifully balanced and very expensive dessert wines, such as mature Riesling, Eiswein, Tokaji, and Port, that can age for ages. Sip some if you ever get the chance.

So expect some age on big reds and some well-made whites. Also, remember never to be intimidated by so-called experts who tell you that all wine has to age a long time before you consume it. Some people say the same thing about cheese, but we know better.

DETECTING FAULTS OR FLAWS

As with so many other good things in life, wine can suffer from bad handling and storage. Wine is alive, just as we are, and it can get sick, too, even die, just as we can. If you learn the few illnesses it can have, you'll be ahead of the game by being able to recognize those faults and flaws.

According to my copy of the 2010 *New Oxford American Dictionary,* a *fault* is an unattractive or unsatisfactory feature. The word *flaw* is defined as a fault or other imperfection that mars a substance. Sounds pretty much the same to me. In my book, therefore, *faults* are *flaws* and *flaws* are *faults* (please don't set the dictionary police on me).

You should also know that many wine drinkers, even so-called experts, couldn't detect even the most obvious fault-flaw if their noses fell off into the glass. It's all a matter of sensitivity to smell. However, stay with me; it's not very hard to figure out when the wine you're smelling is off (not good) or worse.

1. **If the wine looks strange,** it probably is off. A wine that's supposed to be red, but isn't, should make you suspicious. A wine that's supposed to be white (or pale yellow), but is dark or brown or both, is definitely off. Don't drink either one. (This doesn't apply to aged vintage Port or aged Sherry, which can, and often does, have strange dark colors.)

2. **Do you notice things floating in it,** other than small bits of harmless cork that fell in during cork removal, or tiny crystals on the bottom of your glass or bottle? These crystals, called *tartrates* (from tartaric acid), are just harmless by-products of fermentation. Don't worry about them.

3. **If the wine smells or tastes funky,** like wet cardboard, or like sour, bitter, or rotten produce, it's

probably bad; stay away. It may also have a contaminated cork, ruined by a vile chemical called TCA (don't ask). Or the off-smell may simply be mold or other contamination you'd want to avoid. Do so.

Some experts estimate that 3–10 percent of all natural corks in wine bottles are contaminated or leak (bad). Which is why we also take a good healthy sniff of the wine before we taste it, and when we taste, we only take a tiny sip first. Get into the habit of smelling and tasting the wine carefully before pouring it into the glasses. Better for you to detect a bad bottle than for your dinner guests to discover something amiss, no?

Even though a bad wine usually won't kill you, it sure can ruin a lovely dinner or evening. Now that you're privy to some of the darker secrets of wine, you'll be prepared.

TIP: In some restaurants, the wine may be opened by the wine server (also called the *sommelier;* som-el-YAY, the French word for wine captain or steward). Then the cork, which has already just been smelled by the sommelier, is placed on the table before you. In the good old days, you picked it up and sniffed it to see if all was well. Today, just look at the cork to see if there has been leakage (bad) or that the name stamped on the cork is consistent with the front label (good). Don't bother to sniff it, but simply wait for a small tasting sample to be poured into your glass. If, after a sniff and taste, the wine seems healthy and/or normal, you should nod and say something like, "Fine" or "Okay." Leave the cork alone or set it aside somewhere. Cork-sniffing by a customer in a restaurant is no longer necessary and has become just another dead tradition.

(P.S. Sniffing a genuine cork at home is okay since you're the one opening the bottle. Sniffing a plastic cork or screw cap is not only unnecessary but just plain silly.)

MATCHING WINE WITH FOOD

Of course, you've heard the old adage, *white with fish, red with meat.* How about which wine with spicy Thai or Vietnamese food, fresh spring asparagus, eggs, cheeseburgers, birthday cake, sausages with sauerkraut, stinky cheese, Caesar salad, chocolate desserts, and the other thousands of different foods we all eat daily?

Not to worry. I won't make you memorize every perfect combination of food and wine. Just simple rules that'll cover a lot of foods.

Remember when we talked about *body, weight,* and *mouthfeel* earlier? One good rule to remember, if there is a rule, is that when matching food and wine, light wine goes with light food and heavy wine goes with heavy food; dry wine goes with savory (or nonsweet) food; sweet wine goes with sweet food/desserts. (Off-dry or slightly sweet wines go well with spicy foods.)

Also, remember another important caveat when matching food and wine: drink local wines with local foods; they always go well together. However, if all else fails, drink a sparkling high-acid wine, such as Champagne, Cava, Prosecco, Asti, whatever. It'll usually do the trick.

The hard part of matching food and wine usually occurs in restaurants when each person at the table is ordering a different dish: light/heavy, hot/cold, bland/spicy, meat/vegetarian, summery/wintery, classic/cutting edge. This is the perfect time to encourage all the guests to order wine by the glass, for as many glasses as they want. It may cost more than full bottles, but at least all of you will get the wine you prefer. Saves a lot of half-full bottles and shocking bills at the end

There are some other things you should learn about the order of wines in a meal: a sparkling wine is always a fine way to start a fine meal; then something light—red or white, or even a rosé—with soup or another appetizer; for the entrée, a substantial white or red. For cheese or nuts, perhaps a good Port; for a sweet, rich dessert, a sweet, rich wine such as a Sauternes, or an ice wine from Germany or Canada, or perhaps a *sticky*, the wonderful dessert wine from Australia. Try everything you can; the more you experience the better able you'll be to make a good match, possibly even one in food-and-wine heaven.

Speaking of culinary bliss, lots and lots of experience has confirmed some excellent matches that have become classics:

> chili or hamburgers with red Zinfandel
> chocolate with Port
> lamb with red Bordeaux
> lobster with white Burgundy or Chardonnay
> shellfish with Muscadet, Chablis, or Sancerre
> pasta in tomato sauce with Chianti
> prosciutto with Pinot Grigio
> roast chicken with Chardonnay
> roast duck or ham with Pinot Noir
> salmon with Pinot Noir
> spicy Asian food with off-dry Riesling
> steak with Cabernet Sauvignon

One final warning on matching wine with food: some foods just refuse to cooperate with some wines, so it's best to avoid the problems altogether by choosing other things to eat or drink. These food culprits are usually artichokes, asparagus, eggs, and vinegary salads.

Try some combos yourself to see what works and what doesn't. That way, you won't be stumped when the time comes to pair up the liquids and the solids.

ORDERING WINE OUT

There are few things more unpleasant to an adult new to wine than being asked to select the wine at your table in a restaurant. Eek! What to do?

First, do a little homework. On the Internet, check the wine menu of the restaurant you're planning to go to. This way you won't panic when you're finally seated at the restaurant; just relax, smile, and then ask everyone at the table (nicely) what they're ordering: seafood, steak, pasta, salad, whatever. If there's light stuff and heavy-duty stuff, you'll quickly have to figure on something light or white and something heavy or red. At least a bottle of each for two-to-four people.

Also, don't be intimidated by a (usually helpful but sometimes snobby) sommelier. These professionals are highly trained and experienced in matching wines to foods, especially in their own restaurants. Be friendly and ask for their advice; they only want you to have a pleasant dinner and to come back again and again. Trust their judgment and thank them for their help with a gratuity at the end of a lovely dining experience if you're pleased with what they suggested.

However, be somewhat on your guard: there are still some aggressive sommeliers out there who'll try to upsell you, that is, try to sell you something quite a bit more expensive than you're comfortable with. Just stand your ground and say something like, "No, thanks. I'll stay with my choice" or "I'll still go with the house wine."

When you do finally order a bottle of wine, make sure the vintage (the year) on the label is the same as the one on the wine list; most times they are, sometimes they're not.

Remember, too, that all sommeliers need to know what everybody is ordering and, if possible, your financial limitations. You can say something like: "We'd like a young red that's a good value," or "We'd like a really fine white with our crab starter and a well-aged red for our strip steaks."

Wine comes in a variety of quantities in a restaurant: as little as a glass, a small carafe, decanter or half bottle (375 milliliters) that's usually fine for one or two people, a full bottle (750 milliliters), or a magnum (1,500 milliliters or two bottles' worth). If all the people at your table are having something different, let everybody order a glass or two of whatever is available. Wine by the glass is also a good idea if there's only a server and no wine manager around to help you. The waitstaff in most restaurants aren't as knowledgeable as wine professionals, nor should they be.

If, oh no, there's no one to help you select the wines and you only have the wine list to work with, take another deep breath and first scan the list for prices to find your monetary comfort zone. Just don't select the two very cheapest wines listed, red or white. They're put there by some cynical restaurant owners who want to trick you into buying something much more expensive (these two cheapies are often nearly undrinkable swill bought by the tanker). Should everything else fail, order the house red or white; either is usually okay and sometimes quite good, not to mention a lot less costly.

The more you study wine, the more confident you'll become in ordering what you want and what your dining companions would enjoy. The only downer to a fun evening is for you to get paralyzed with indecision; that would be uncomfortable for everyone at your table.

The whole point is to have a good time in a restaurant, whether there are only two of you or a whole rowdy bunch enjoying a happy occasion.

SHOPPING FOR WINE

Next to ordering wine in a restaurant, picking out a wine in a store is the next most frightening situation for a beginner. There really is only one solution to this problem: ask questions. ask, ask, and ask again. Never stop asking and trying different wines so you can navigate with the best of them. Here are some tips:

1. **Find a wine store where you're comfortable,** where the staff is helpful, and where wine is respected (not a glorified beverage warehouse outlet that carries a few labels of cheap wine as a feeble attempt at diversity). Also, be on the lookout in any beverage store where the bottles of wine, including their display racks, are dirty or displayed in a hot window. This is a tipoff that it's best to avoid buying anything there, particularly wine. Also, an unkempt wine store is a clear signal that the owners and managers of the store don't really give a damn about wine. Try another store.

2. **Cultivate any employee who is helpful and knowl-edgeable.** Ask questions; there are no dumb questions about wine, only surly or condescending answers from unpleasant people.

3. **Continue to visit and buy from the same store,** so the staff gets to know you better. If they love wine, and love to talk about it, pick their brains.

4. **Tell them the kind of wines you prefer,** and a com-fortable price level for your everyday preferences. Ask about special-occasion wines or appropriate wines to bring as a house gift. Find out if and when the retailer has wine tastings and try to attend some to become better acquainted with what they're pouring. The more you taste, the better your skills.

5. **Don't forget to ask about special store promotions or discounts,** or even special buys that haven't yet been advertised. You can save some nice money when you make a friend who works in the store.

6. **Once you get the hang of selecting and buying wine in a retail store,** you may also try buying wine on the Internet. Don't expect much, if any, personal attention, as you may get in a store. You're shopping for the best price or you're trying to find something unavailable in your local store. In addition, remember that the shipping charges may wipe out any savings over the price in your local store.

7. **Finally, there's really no magic to buying wine.** Knowledge and familiarity with the wine is just the result of a little experience and some common sense. One of the nice aspects of getting recognized at a wine store and interacting with the staff is that they're usually willing to help with suggestions about matching wine to food. Trust their experience and taste until yours is better developed. A trusting relationship with a good wine store employee will pay many dividends in the years to come.

While picking up favorites, also pick up some new labels; wines from unfamiliar grapes; other vineyards, regions, or countries. You just might discover a great new taste, a great new bottle or two to share with friends. The beauty of wine is that there are so many out there, so many new ones to try, but not enough time to try them all. That's called the wine lover's dilemma.

A final note: did you know that more women than men buy wine in stores, but that more men than women order wine in restaurants? Why is that?

Doesn't matter a bit to me as long as I get to taste new wines with old friends, or old wines with new friends.

WHAT TO BRING AS A GUEST

The rules for being a gracious guest is the other side of being a gracious host or hostess: know what's being served beforehand. Easy-peasy.

If you call the host a few days ahead of time, you should be able to gather the information you need about the meal and the number of people expected. You can tell the party-giver that you'll bring some or all of the wine, if that's okay. Your budget will fill in the blanks. Just make sure you talk with a trusted wine merchant and work out the types and number of bottles, at least one (boo) or a case of twelve (hooray), or even a half-case (okay). Refresh your memory about matching wines to food so you'll be able to arrive with a welcome gift.

When you do get to the dinner party, just present the wine(s) without a lot of fuss and leave it to the hosts to open. Never insist that they open the wine you brought; let them decide what to serve in their own home. Should you bring a wine below their standards, don't be insulted if they serve their own wine instead. Be better prepared the next time. Your job is over, so don't sulk; just go enjoy yourself.

A key point to remember here is that one bottle of a good wine is *always*, repeat *always,* better than two or more bottles of something you found in the closeout bin in the wine store. Sheer quantity is rarely appreciated except at a postgame party in the dorm.

SCENARIO 1: Okay, you've called the hosts and found out they're having ten people to a dinner with a crown roast of pork as the entrée. What should you bring? First, don't bother to bring a kosher wine; it will be deeply unappreciated at this porcine celebration. Pork, like veal and chicken, is a white meat, so a perfect match would be Pinot Noir, a light red wine with loads of character and layers of complexity, assuming you bring something decent (at least $20 a bottle). For white wine lovers, bring a dryish German Riesling or a nice, food-loving, lightly oaked Chardonnay. Three bottles of the red and three of the white should be more than enough for twelve; at $20 a bottle, this should set you back about $120, if you can afford it. If not, scale the gift back to one bottle of red and one bottle of white, a total of no less than $40. If things are very tight, just bring the Pinot Noir. However many you bring, you should be greeted with warmth and thanks, and might even get invited back.

SCENARIO 2: A Fourth-of-July backyard barbecue with neighbors, kids, dogs, firecrackers, and a good dose of patriotism. If the 'cue includes grilled shrimp or chicken, bring some good, tart Sauvignon Blanc because it's great with anything from the sea or anything that walked around clucking. A nice American Chard is always appreciated, too. Also, bring some decent red California Zinfandel or a Zin blend to pair with the ribs, burgers, or steaks. Drink the Sauvi and Chard cold and the Zin cool. Help with the cooking and the cleanup. Remember to drink responsibly or find a designated driver. Enjoy yourself: it's America's birthday and, like the old woman who lived in a shoe, we're all her many children.

If all else fails, bring some bottles of a good cold sparkling wine, such as an American Prosecco, yes, American-made Prosecco. It should go fine with just about anything from the grill.

What to bring as a guest isn't mysterious. Just know before you go, so you're tipped off in advance about what'll be served and how many guests there will be, and let common sense prevail.

But remember: if you want to get invited back, never take your unfinished bottles home with you; this is not a restaurant experience.

HOW TO TALK ABOUT WINE, AND TALK, AND TALK, AND TALK, AND TALK, AND TALK, AND TALK, AND TALK, AND TALK

W hy are there so many books, articles, and blogs written about wine, with more and more every day? Is wine so inscrutable that no one could possibly understand it? I suppose it's just another manifestation of the human condition: forever searching for knowledge, always more knowledge, plus the need for language to express it.

This last chapter brings us to the language of wine, that is, how to describe what you smell and taste in wine, how to put words to wine so that they make sense not only to you, but also to others. There's no single path to learning the language of wine, any more than there's a single path to talking about our planet, our environment, the human condition, religion, or any number of big questions out there.

Since we're human, we simply must talk. A lot. It's a condition of our existence and we can't escape it. In this case, we talk about wine because we want to communicate our impressions and sensations to other people who also smell, taste, drink, and talk about wine.

As you now know, wine is a great conjurer that makes us want to describe the sensations we experience with wine. We call wine *good*, we call it *sturdy*, we call it *delicate*, *ripe*, *perfectly aged*, *over the hill*, *mean*, *inspiring*, *gnarly*, *well bred*, *doomed* and on and on and on until eyes glaze over.

We use thousands of descriptors, some *bizarre*, some *erotic*, some *funny*, some *outrageous*, some *poetic* or *silly*, and some *just plain ugly*. Our vocabulary is nearly as limitless when describing a breathtaking sunset, a Mozart piano concerto, a perfect haiku, the smile on a child's face, a lover's caress. Sometimes, there are no words; more often, though, we humans can and will eventually come up with novel ways to describe the indescribable. After all, that's part of what makes us human.

Let your mind wander and then retrieve your stored memories of smells and tastes from the past, as in "Wow, this reminds me of . . ." or "This tastes just like that great Sancerre we had in France . . ." or "Mmm, just like that incredible red we enjoyed in Sonoma."

You've come to the end of this little primer on wine. But not the end of your education. There'll come a point where you'll simply have to go on tasting more and more wines, made from different grapes, vineyards, countries. Once you're hooked on wine, you'll see it through to your very last bottle, and you'll describe it with all the imagination in your new arsenal of wine words.

An important reminder: never forget that you must drink your favorite wine responsibly and in moderation, with loved ones, with family and friends, with people who share your new enthusiasm for . . . life. Because the wine in a bottle is a living, evolving, and unique individual whose journey is only a relatively short one on earth, just like our own.

So enjoy that journey. Enjoy your life and all the delicious wine in it. And never, ever, let anyone intimidate you again because you don't know enough about wine.

Because now you do.

On the next and last page in this book (hooray), you'll find some of the wackiest wine descriptors ever conceived. For the record, I didn't make them up; no one could. They were all taken from thousands upon thousands of legitimate wine reviews by serious wine professionals. (I wonder if they had fun writing them.)

SOME VERY STRANGE WINE-TASTING LANGUAGE

aborigine's armpits, absolute nightmare, all the finesse of a horny hippopotamus, all the subtlety of a chainsaw, **baboon's bottom,** Bangkok paddy field, bathroom mold, bog-standard, boiled crab shells, boiled fruitcake, **camel spit,** carnally perfumed, Château Phlegm '89, chicken fat, confusing blue cheese, crushed ants, **Darth Vader® of a wine,** decayed wombat, diner breakfast, downright ugly, DPIM (Don't Put In Mouth), duck fart, **eggroll wrapper,** elephant cage at the zoo, embalmed, enough tannin to pucker the liver, escargot mud pie, **feral stink of a sun-warmed manure pile,** fermented oak juice, flyblown butcher's shop, Frankenstein Pinot, **gefilte fish,** gerbil cage, glue and bananas, Godzilla®, good for cleaning false teeth, grotty and vile, **Hawaiian volcanic ash-tinged notes of duck's breath,** herb-infused jet fuel, hermaphroditic, hot-dog water, **ice princess,** I could climb into the glass, ignoble rot, industrial Kool-Aid®, intoxicating grape sweat, **James Cagney grapefruit facial,** jam fest, Joseph's coat of many colors, just plain evil, just-used bathroom, **kicking like new-born foals,** kick in the stomach, kicks butt from start to finish, kitchen sink, kitty pee-pee, **laboratory-concocted Stepford wine,** ladies' underwear, like an angel peed on my tongue, liquid ecstasy, **makes the Earth move,** Marie Antoinette's boudoir, may be hazardous to your health, Muzak® for your palate, **Neanderthal-style,** no splinters in the nose, new Vaseline®, Novocaine®-like, new condom smell, not worth hating, **oak bra,** odd-tasting Eastern European fruit soup, old hen droppings, one step up from vinegar, organic waste, **paint stripper,** pickled frog skin, Pinot with training wheels, plastic whiff of Eau de Mattel®, pure sex in a bottle, **quail-egg casserole,** quietly soulful, quince cheese, quintessential nonwine: no bouquet, no

fruit, no flavors, no finish, **raisin massacre,** Rambo®
Champagne, rancid pork, rat poison, road kill, rolling
thunder, rotten fish, rugged sweaty honey, **sap-laden
rocks,** skunk cabbage, soulful barnyard, Spanish loo,
sweaty saddle, sweet odor of cow, **tea and mothballs,**
termite's fantasy dinner, throat sandpaperer, tincture of
vomit, tongue-happy, touch of death, trash-can wine,
undrinkable gloppy butterball, uppity cherries, unswal-
lowable, uriny, use it to kill rats, **velvety and rusty nails,**
very diesel-like, vin de merde, vinous lap-dance, vinous
nose-candy, virile mousse, viscosity of 10W40 motor oil,
wasabi, waxy cadaver, wet underpants, Windex®,
winegasm, wonderfully grouchy, won't shrivel your
tonsils, **yak drool,** YMCA® pool, your horse is diabetic,
your tongue might be confused but it will be happy,
youthful kerosene, **Zen-like,** zigzags across your palate
like a pinball, zillion points from Robert Parker, zingy-
nettley, zwieback